JOSÉ ANTONIO PAGOLA

Following in the Footsteps of Jesus
Meditations on the Gospels for Year A

Translated by Valentine de Souza s.j.

CONVIVIUMPRESS

SERIES MINISTERIA

2010

Following in the Footsteps of Jesus
Meditations on the Gospels for Year A

© José Antonio Pagola

© Convivium Press 2010
All rights reserved
Todos los derechos reservados
For the English Edition

http://www.conviviumpress.com
sales@conviviumpress.com
convivium@conviviumpress.com

7661 NW 68th St, Suite 108,
Miami, Florida 33166. USA.
Phone: +1 (786) 8669718
Fax: +1 (305) 8875463

Edited *by* Rafael Luciani
Translated *by* Valentine de Souza s.J.
Bible translation: New International Version
Designed *by* Eduardo Chumaceiro d'E
Series: *Ministeria*

ISBN: 978-1-934996-23-2

Printed in Colombia
Impreso en Colombia
D'VINNI, S.A.

Convivium Press
Miami, 2010

Following in the Footsteps of Jesus

Meditations on the Gospels for Year A

Contents

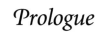 *Prologue*

Christianity it would seem is, with notable exceptions, an exercise in being Christian without following Christ. «The Christian ideal has not been tried and found wanting. It has been found difficult and left untried» (G.K. Chesterton).

These meditations teach us what following Christ entails and exactly why living the Christian ideal is difficult, why it is left untried. The author, José Antonio Pagola, explains:

> What makes us Christian is to follow Jesus. That's all. This following of Jesus is not theoretical or abstract. It means following in his footsteps, committing ourselves to humanizing life and so contributing little by little to making a reality of his project of a world where God and his justice reign.

This means that we, the followers of Jesus, are sent to bring truth where there is deceit and lies; to bring justice where there is injustice and cruelty to the weakest; to bring back compassion where there is indifference and passivity at the sight of those who suffer. This entails building communities that unite on the basis of the project of Jesus while living his spirit and attitudes.

Sooner or later, following Jesus brings with it conflicts, problems and suffering. One must be ready to face reactions and resistance from those who for one reason or another do not want a more human world, like the kind that God wants as revealed by Jesus. They want something else.

The Gospels have preserved a realistic call of Jesus to his followers. The shock his metaphorical image carries with it can only come from him: *If someone wants to come after me... let him take up his cross and follow me.* Jesus does not deceive them. If they really follow him, they will have to suffer his fate. They will end up like him. That will be the final proof that they have been faithful in following him.

To follow Jesus is an all-consuming task. It is difficult to imagine a more noble or dignified life. But it has its price. To follow Jesus it is important to «do»: to create a world that is more just; to build a church more faithful to the Gospels. Yet it is just as important, or more so, to «suffer» in order to bring about a more just world, to suffer for a church more faithful to the Gospels.

VALENTINE DE SOUZA S.J.

Introduction

I am the Vine; you are the branches.

The image is extraordinarily powerful. Jesus is the vine, and we who believe in him are the branches. The vitality of Christians derives from him. If the sap of the Risen Jesus flows into our lives, it will bring us joy, light, creativity, and courage to live like him. If, on the other hand, it does not flow in us, we will become like dry branches.

This is the real problem: the church celebrates the Risen Jesus as a vine full of life, but it is largely made up of dead branches. Why are we engaged in so many activities, if the spirit of Jesus does not flow in our communities and in our hearts?

Our main task today and always is to remain in the vine, not to live separate from Jesus, not to be deprived of the sap, not to dry up again. How do we do this? The gospel says it clearly: we must take care that his message remains alive in us.

Christian life does not arise spontaneously in us. The truth of the gospel cannot always be reached through a process of reasoning. We need to meditate long on the words of Jesus. It is only through familiarity and association with the Gospels that we begin slowly to learn to live like him.

This close familiarity with the words of the Gospels brings us into consonance with Jesus, inspires in us his love for the world, builds up enthusiasm for his project of the Kingdom of God, and infuses his spirit in us. Without our scarcely noticing it we become Christian.

This personal meditation on the words of Jesus transforms us more than all the explanations, sermons, and exhortations that reach us from the outside. People change from within. Perhaps one of the most serious problems of our religion is that we do not change, because only what flows through our hearts changes our lives, and frequently it is not the vital sap of Jesus that passes through our hearts.

The life of the church would be transformed if believers, Christian couples, priests, religious, bishops and educators would make the Gospels their bedside book.

JOSÉ ANTONIO PAGOLA

Part one

Advent

1

Awakening

> *«Therefore keep watch, because you do not know on what day your Lord will come. But understand this: If the owner of the house had known at what time of night the thief was coming, he would have kept watch and would not have let his house be broken into. So you also must be ready, because the Son of Man will come at an hour when you do not expect him».*

One day the dramatic story of humankind will end, as life inevitably ends for each one of us. The Gospels mention a discourse of Jesus on the end of all things, and they always highlight his warning to be watchful, to be alert, to stay awake. The first generations of Christians gave great importance to this watchfulness. As the end of the world did not come as quickly as some expected, they saw the risk of slowly forgetting Jesus and did not want him to find them asleep one day.

Since then many centuries have passed. How do Christians live today? Are we awake or have we slowly gone to sleep? Are we deeply attracted to Jesus or are we distracted by all sorts of side issues? Do we follow him or have we learned to live like the rest of the world?

To watch is first and foremost to awaken from unawareness. We live an illusion of being Christian, when in fact quite often our interests, attitudes and way of living are not those of Jesus. This illusion shields us from seeking our personal conversion and that of the church. Without «awakening», we will continue deceiving ourselves.

To watch is to live with the awareness of reality; to listen to the groaning of those who suffer; to know the love of God for life; to live more in touch with his coming into our lives, into our society, into this world of ours. Without this kind of sensitivity it is not possible to follow in the footsteps of Jesus.

We live immune to the challenges of the gospel. We do have hearts, but they have hardened. We have our ears open, but we do not hear what Jesus heard. We have our eyes open, but we do not see life as Jesus saw it; we do not see people as Jesus saw them. Could what Jesus wanted to avoid happen among his disciples —that they are seen like «the blind leading the blind»?

If we do not awaken, could it happen that we too would ask with those people at the last judgment who in the parable asked: *«Lord, when did we see you hungry or thirsty, a stranger or naked or sick or in prison and did not help you?»*

2

Sustained Conversion

MATTHEW 3: 1-12

SECOND SUNDAY OF ADVENT

«In those days John the Baptist came, preaching in the Desert of Judea and saying, "Repent, for the kingdom of heaven is near". This is he who was spoken of through the prophet Isaiah: "A voice of one calling in the desert: Prepare the way for the Lord, make straight paths for him".

John's clothes were made of camel's hair and he had a leather belt around his waist. His food was locusts and wild honey. People went out to him from Jerusalem and all Judea and the whole region of the Jordan. Confessing their sins, they were baptized by him in the Jordan River».

Between the autumn of the year 27 and spring of 28 there appeared on the religious horizon of Palestine an original and independent prophet who had a strong impact on the people. His name was John. The first generation of Christians always saw him as the man who prepared the way for Jesus.

There is something new and surprising in this prophet. He does not preach in Jerusalem like Isaiah and the other prophets; he lived apart from the elite of the temple. Nor is he a prophet of the court; he moves far away from the palace of Herod Antipas. About him it was said that he was «a voice crying in the desert», a place that cannot be easily controlled by any power.

The decrees of Rome do not reach as far as the desert; neither do the orders of Herod. The din and bustle of the temple is not heard there; neither do they hear the discussions of the teachers on the Law. Instead, one can listen to God in silence and solitude. It is the best place to begin turning to God, to begin preparing the way to Jesus.

This is precisely the message of John: «*Repent; prepare the way of the Lord, make straight his paths*». This «way of the Lord» is not the Roman roads through which the legions of Tiberius march. These paths are no avenues leading to the temple. We need to open new paths to God that come with Jesus.

The first thing we need again today is to convert ourselves to God, to return to Jesus, to open paths to him in the world and in the church. It isn't a question of updating or of adaptation to the present time. It is much more. It means placing the whole church in a state of conversion.

It will probably take a long time to put compassion at the heart of Christianity. It won't be easy to move from a «religion of authority» to a «religion of vocation». It will be years before Christian communities learn to live for God's kingdom and his righteousness. Profound changes will be needed in order to place the poor at the center of our religion. One can only follow Jesus while in a state of conversion. We need to foster a sustained conversion, an attitude of conversion

that we transmit to future generations. Only such a church is
worthy of Jesus.

3

The Identity of Christ

MATTHEW 11: 2-11

THIRD SUNDAY OF ADVENT

> «*When John heard in prison what Christ was doing, he sent his
> disciples to ask him, "Are you the one who was to come, or should
> we expect someone else?" Jesus replied, "Go back and report to
> John what you hear and see: The blind receive sight, the lame
> walk, those who have leprosy are cured, the deaf hear, the dead
> are raised, and the good news is preached to the poor. Blessed is
> the man who does not fall away on account of me"*».

In his prison cell up in the stronghold of Machaerus where
he is confined by Herod, news of Jesus reaches John. He is
baffled by what he hears. Jesus does not meet his expectations. He expected a Messiah who would impose himself
with the terrible force of the judgment of God, saving those
who accepted his baptism and condemning those who rejected it. Who is Jesus?

To get rid of his doubts, John sends two disciples to ask Jesus
about his true identity: «*Are you the one who was to come or
should we expect someone else?*» The question was decisive in
the early days of Christianity. Jesus' response is not theoretical
but very practical and precise: «*Go back to John and report what
you hear and see*». They ask for his identity and Jesus responds
with his healing work, his serving the sick, the poor and unfortunate people whom he finds in the villages of Galilee, without
resources or hope for a better life: «*The blind receive sight, the
lame walk, those who have leprosy are cured, the deaf hear, the
dead are raised, and the good news is preached to the poor*».

To know Jesus, it is best to see whom he approaches and what he loves to do. To understand clearly his identity, it is not enough to acknowledge theoretically that he is the Messiah, the Son of God. One must also identify with his way of being the Messiah, which is nothing less than to relieve suffering, to heal lives, and to open a horizon of hope for the poor.

Jesus knows that his answer may disappoint those who dream of a powerful Messiah, a judge who condemns human beings. So he adds: *«Happy is he who will not feel let down by me»*. Do not expect another Messiah to act differently; let no one invent another Christ more to his liking, because the Son was sent to make life more dignified and happy for everyone, something that will be fulfilled completely in the final feast of the Father.

Which Messiah do we Christians follow today? Do we love to do the things that Jesus did? And if we do not do these things, what are we doing in the midst of the world? What are people «seeing and hearing» in the church of Jesus? What do they see in our lives? What do they hear in our words?

4
The Name of Jesus

MATTHEW 1: 18-24

FOURTH SUNDAY OF ADVENT

«This is how the birth of Jesus Christ came about: His mother Mary was pledged to be married to Joseph, but before they came together, she was found to be with child through the Holy Spirit. Because Joseph her husband was a righteous man and did not want to expose her to public disgrace, he had in mind to divorce her quietly. But after he had considered this, an angel of the Lord appeared to him in a dream and said, "Joseph son of David, do not be afraid to take Mary home as your wife, because what is conceived in her is from the Holy Spirit. She will give birth to a

son, and you are to give him the name Jesus, because he will save his people from their sins".

All this took place to fulfill what the Lord had said through the prophet: "The virgin will be with child and will give birth to a son, and they will call him Immanuel" —which means, "God with us". When Joseph woke up, he did what the angel of the Lord had commanded him and took Mary home as his wife».

A person was not given a name arbitrarily among the Hebrews, because the «name», as in almost all ancient cultures, represents a person's being, his true identity, what is expected of him or her.

So the evangelist Matthew is very keen from the beginning to explain to his readers the profound meaning of the name of the person of whom he is going to speak throughout his Gospel. The «name» of that child not yet born is «Jesus», which means «God saves». He is so named because *«he will save his people from their sins»*.

In the year 70 Vespasian, appointed as the new emperor while he was putting down the Jewish revolt, marches toward Rome, where he is welcomed and acclaimed by two names: «savior» and «benefactor». The evangelist Matthew wants to make things clear. The «savior» the world needs is not Vespasian but Jesus.

Salvation will not come to us from any emperor or any victory of one people over another. Humanity needs to be saved from evil, injustice and violence; it needs to be pardoned and to be reoriented toward a more dignified life for human beings. This is the salvation offered to us in Jesus.

Matthew also assigns him a new name: «Emmanuel». He knows that Jesus has not been named thus historically. The name is shocking, absolutely new, and means «God with us», a name that only we who believe in Jesus attribute to him as due to him. God is with us, blesses us and saves us.

The first Christian generations bore the name of Jesus imprinted in their hearts. They repeat it again and again. They are baptized in his name, they gather to pray in his name. For Matthew, it is an ardent synthesis of his faith. For Paul, there is nothing bigger. According to one of the earliest Christian hymns, *«before the name of Jesus every knee must bend»*.

After twenty centuries, we must learn to take the name of Jesus in a new way —with affection and love, with renewed faith, in a spirit of conversion. With his name on our lips and in our hearts we can live and die with hope.

Advent

Part two

Christmas Season

1

The Heart of Christmas

THE NATIVITY

«*And there were shepherds living out in the fields nearby, keeping watch over their flocks at night. An angel of the Lord appeared to them, and the glory of the Lord shone around them, and they were terrified. But the angel said to them, "Do not be afraid. I bring you good news of great joy that will be for all the people. Today in the town of David a Savior has been born to you; he is Christ the Lord. This will be a sign to you: You will find a baby wrapped in cloths and lying in a manger"*».

We participate in some wonderful celebrations without knowing exactly why they exist. We exchange greetings and do not know what they are for. We celebrate Christmas, but its meaning is hidden from us. Many do not even remember the purpose of these celebrations. Therefore, why not listen to the «first announcement» of Christmas which the evangelist Luke wrote in about the year 80.

It is a dark night, so the story goes. Some shepherds are suddenly enveloped by a bright glow. The scene is one of grandeur: the night is lit up by what the evangelist calls the «*glory of the Lord*». However, the shepherds «*were terrified*». It is not the comfortable darkness that they fear, but the unexpected light. Hence the announcement begins with these words: «*Do not be afraid*».

We must not be surprised by those words. We too prefer to live in our accustomed darkness, because we fear the light of God. We do not want to live in the truth, but those who do not introduce more light and truth into their lives in these days, will not truly celebrate Christmas.

The messenger continues, «*I bring you good news of great joy that will be for all the people*». The joy of Christmas is not one among others. It is not to be confused with any kind of well-being, satisfaction or enjoyment. It is an unmistakably great joy that comes from the «*good news*» of Jesus. Hence it is «*for all the people*» and must reach especially those who suffer and live lives filled with sadness.

If Jesus is not «good news» for us, if his gospel means nothing to us, if we do not know the joy that only God can give us, or if we reduce these events to everyone merely enjoying their prosperity or to selfish, comfortable religiosity, we will be celebrating anything but Christmas.

The only reason to celebrate is because «*Today a Savior has been born to you*». That child has not only been born to Mary and Joseph; he belongs to all of us. He is «the Savior» of the world, the only one in whom we can place our final hope. The world as we know it is not the absolute reality. Jesus Christ is the hope that the injustice that contaminates everything today will not last forever.

We may experience very fine emotions, enjoy our homes and friendships; they will give us moments of happiness. All that is fine, but that is still not Christmas. Only with the hope offered by Jesus Christ is there truly Christmas.

2

A Son of Immigrants

MATTHEW 2:13-15, 19-23

THE HOLY FAMILY

> «*When they had gone, an angel of the Lord appeared to Joseph in a dream. "Get up, he said, take the child and his mother and escape to Egypt. Stay there until I tell you, for Herod is going to search for the child to kill him". So he got up, took the child and his mother during the night and left for Egypt, where he stayed*

*until the death of Herod. And so was fulfilled what the Lord
had said through the prophet: Out of Egypt I called my son».*

*«After Herod died, an angel of the Lord appeared in a
dream to Joseph in Egypt and said, Get up, take the child and
his mother and go to the land of Israel, for those who were trying to take the child's life are dead. So he got up, took the child
and his mother and went to the land of Israel. But when he
heard that Archelaus was reigning in Judea in place of his father Herod, he was afraid to go there. Having been warned in a
dream, he withdrew to the district of Galilee. And he went and
lived in a town called Nazareth. So was fulfilled what was said
through the prophets: "He will be called a Nazarene"».*

Ordinarily Christians imagine Mary and Joseph enjoying the
company of their son Jesus in their little home in Nazareth in
an enviable atmosphere of peace and happiness. This is not
the picture that the evangelist Matthew gives us of the holy
family. His somber account of the early years of Jesus shat-
ters all the fantasies we build around Christmas.

According to Matthew, Jesus' family could not live in peace.
Herod wants to kill the child so one day he would not snatch
his power from him. Joseph has to act fast. The danger is imminent. Take the child and his mother «*at night*», and, without waiting for a new dawn, «*flee to Egypt*».

The journey is hard and dangerous. Mary and Joseph
remember the hardships endured by their people in that
same desert. Now they are reliving them with their son Jesus.
The three are seeking asylum in a foreign country far from
home and from their people. All is uncertainty and insecu-
rity. They don't know when they will be able to return. They
will be told.

After Herod's death, the family breathes a sigh of relief
and begins the journey back home. But Archelaus reigns in
Judea, a man who according to the historian, Flavius Josephus,
was known for his cruelty and tyranny. Joseph «*is afraid*». It
is not a safe place for Jesus. They will move to Galilee and set-

tle down in Nazareth, a village lost in the mountains, which, so far, seems a less dangerous place.

It is in this way that the holy family lives, protecting their son so he can survive, migrating from one place to another in search of bread and work, homeless and insecure in a land dominated by powerful «kings» such as Herod or Archelaus.

The great news of Christmas is that God was not born to the privileged of the earth, to celebrate his coming with tables loaded with dinner and superfluous gifts. He was born to share our lives, bringing hope to those who cannot expect much from anyone except God.

3

Mary, Mother of God

LUKE 2: 16-21

BEFOR A NEW YEAR

> «So they hurried off and found Mary and Joseph, and the baby, who was lying in the manger. When they had seen him, they spread the word concerning what had been told them about this child, and all who heard it were amazed at what the shepherds said to them. But Mary treasured up all these things and pondered them in her heart. The shepherds returned, glorifying and praising God for all the things they had heard and seen, which were just as they had been told.
>
> On the eighth day, when it was time to circumcise him, he was named Jesus, the name the angel had given him before he had been conceived».

The theologian Ladislao Boros in one of his writings says that one of the cardinal principles of the Christian life is that «God always begins again». With him, nothing is irrevocably lost. Everything begins and is renewed in him. To put it simply, God is not discouraged by our mediocrity. The renewing strength of his forgiveness and of his grace is more powerful than our errors and sins. With him, everything can begin again.

Therefore, it is good to begin the year with a resolve to start anew. Every year of life granted to us is a time open to new possibilities, a time of grace and salvation in which we are invited to live in a new way. For that, it is important to listen to the questions that may arise from within us.

What do I hope for from the new year? Will it be a year given to doing things, settling affairs, piling up tensions, getting keyed up, living in a bad mood, or will it be a year in which I learn to live a more human life?

What is it that I really want this year? To what will I dedicate my time, which is so valuable and important? Will it once again be a futile, routine and superficial year, or a year in which I will embrace life with joy and gratitude?

How much time will I set aside for rest, for silence, music, prayer, finding God? Will I nurture my interior life, or will I remain overwrought, constantly busy, rushing from one thing to another, without knowing what I want or what I live for?

How much time will I give to enjoying intimacy with my partner, to sharing joyful times with the children? Will I live away from my home, doing as I please, or will I learn to love my own people with greater tenderness and commitment?

With whom will I associate this year? With whom will I come close? Will I give them joy, life, hope, or will I spread discouragement, sorrow, even death? Wherever I have lived, will life there be more joyful and bearable, or harder and more painful?

Will I live this year worried only about my petty well-being, or will I also be concerned about making others happier? Will I be locked into my old, usual selfishness, or will I creatively strive to build around me a more human world, more fit to live in?

Will I continue to live with my back to God, or will I have the courage to believe that he is my best friend? Will I remain silent before him without opening my lips or my heart, or will there at last emerge from an inner recess within me a humble and sincere prayer?

4

Whom Do We Worship?

MATTHEW 2:1-12

EPIPHANY

«*After Jesus was born in Bethlehem in Judea, during the time of King Herod, Magi from the east came to Jerusalem and asked, "Where is the one who has been born king of the Jews? We saw his star in the east and have come to worship him". When King Herod heard this he was disturbed, and all Jerusalem with him. When he had called together all the people's chief priests and teachers of the law, he asked them where the Christ was to be born. "In Bethlehem in Judea", they replied, "for this is what the prophet has written: 'But you, Bethlehem, in the land of Judah, are by no means least among the rulers of Judah; for out of you will come a ruler who will be the shepherd of my people Israel'". Then Herod called the Magi secretly and found out from them the exact time the star had appeared. He sent them to Bethlehem and said, "Go and make a careful search for the child. As soon as you find him, report to me, so that I too may go and worship him".*

After they had heard the king, they went on their way, and the star they had seen in the east went ahead of them until it stopped over the place where the child was. When they saw the star, they were overjoyed. On coming to the house, they saw the child with his mother Mary, and they bowed down and worshiped him. Then they opened their treasures and presented him with gifts of gold and of incense and of myrrh. And having been warned in a dream not to go back to Herod, they returned to their country by another route».

The Magi come from the East, a place that evoked among Jews the home of astrology and other mysterious sciences. They are pagans. They do not know the Holy Scriptures of Israel, but all too well the language of the stars. They are looking for the truth and set out to find it. They are guided by the mysterious and feel the need to «worship».

Their presence causes a flutter in all Jerusalem. The Magi have seen a new star shine that makes them think that a «king of the Jews» has been born and they have come to «worship» him. This king is not Caesar Augustus. Neither is he Herod. Where is he? This is their question.

Herod was startled. The news does not make him very happy. It is he who has been appointed «king of the Jews» by Rome. The newborn king must be done away with. Where is this strange rival? The «chief priests and scribes» know the Scriptures and know that he will be born in Bethlehem, but they do not care about the child nor do they set out to worship him.

This is what Jesus will find throughout his life: hostility and rejection by the representatives of political power, indifference and resistance in religious leaders. Only those who seek God's kingdom and His righteousness will welcome him.

The Magi continued their long search. Sometimes, the star that guides them leaves them in uncertainty. At other times, it shines again filling them with *«great joy»*. Finally they find the Child, and *«falling on their knees, worship him»*. Then, they place at his service the wealth they have and the most valuable treasures they possess. This child can count on them as they recognize him as their King and Lord.

In its apparent simplicity, this story presents us with crucial questions: before whom do we kneel in worship? Which is the God we worship in the depths of our beings? We call ourselves Christians, but do we live in adoration of the Child of Bethlehem? Do we place at his feet our wealth and our prosperity? Are we ready to heed his call to enter the kingdom of God and His righteousness? In our lives there is always a star that guides us towards Bethlehem.

5
The Good Spirit of God

MATTHEW 3:13-17

BAPTISM OF THE LORD

«Then Jesus came from Galilee to the Jordan to be baptized by John. But John tried to deter him, saying, "I need to be baptized by you, and do you come to me?" Jesus replied, "Let it be so now; it is proper for us to do this to fulfill all righteousness". Then John consented. As soon as Jesus was baptized, he went up out of the water. At that moment heaven was opened, and he saw the Spirit of God descending like a dove and lighting on him. And a voice from heaven said, "This is my Son, whom I love; with him I am well pleased"».

Jesus is not hollow or scatterbrained. He does not go about the villages of Galilee acting whimsically or doing his own thing. The Gospels make it clear from the beginning that Jesus lives and acts moved by «the Spirit of God».

The evangelists do not want him to be taken for any «scribe», concerned with bringing about more order in the ways of Israel. He does not want to be identified with a false prophet, willing to seek a balance between religion and the power of Rome.

The evangelist Matthew wants, moreover, to emphasize that no one should equate Jesus with the Baptist; that no one should see him as a mere disciple and collaborator of the great prophet of the desert. Jesus is «the beloved Son» of God. The Spirit of God comes down on him. Only he can «baptize» with the Holy Spirit and with fire.

According to the whole of biblical tradition, the «Spirit of God» is the breath of God that creates, envelops and sustains all life, the power that God has to renew and transform all living beings, and his loving zeal that is always seeking the best for his children.

So Jesus feels he is sent, not to condemn, destroy or curse, but to heal, build up and bless. The Spirit of God leads him to enhance and improve life. Full of that good «Spirit» of God, he devotes himself to ridding the world of evil spirits who do nothing but harm, enslave and dehumanize people.

The first generations of Christians were very clear about what Jesus had been. They summarized the impression he had left etched in the memory of his followers in these words, *«anointed by God with the Holy Spirit…, spent his life doing good and healing all those oppressed by the devil, because God was with him»*.

What is the «spirit» that animates us today as followers of Jesus? What is the «passion» that drives the church? What is the charisma by which believers live and act in our communities? What is it that we bring to the world? If the Spirit of Jesus is in us, we will be «healing» people who are oppressed, depressed, repressed, and even suppressed by evil.

Part three

Lent

Resisting Temptation

MATTHEW 4: 1-11

FIRST SUNDAY OF LENT

«*Then Jesus was led by the Spirit into the desert to be tempted by the devil. After fasting forty days and forty nights, he was hungry. The tempter came to him and said, "If you are the Son of God, tell these stones to become bread". Jesus answered, "It is written: 'Man does not live on bread alone, but on every word that comes from the mouth of God'". Then the devil took him to the holy city and had him stand on the highest point of the temple. "If you are the Son of God", he said, "throw yourself down. For it is written: 'He will command his angels concerning you, and they will lift you up in their hands, so that you will not strike your foot against a stone'". Jesus answered him, "It is also written: 'Do not put the Lord your God to the test'". Again, the devil took him to a very high mountain and showed him all the kingdoms of the world and their splendor. "All this I will give you" he said, "if you will bow down and worship me". Jesus said to him, "Away from me, Satan! For it is written: 'Worship the Lord your God, and serve him only'". Then the devil left him, and angels came and attended him*».

The first temptation takes place in the desert. After fasting «forty days», longing for an encounter with God, Jesus feels hungry. It is then that the tempter suggests turning his attention on himself and to forget God's plans for him. «*If you are the Son of God, tell these stones to become bread*».

Jesus, exhausted but full of the Spirit of God, reacts: «*Man does not live on bread alone, but on every word that comes from the mouth of God*». He will not be looking to his own interests. He will not be an egoistical Messiah. He will multiply bread when he sees the poor hungry. He will be nourished by the living word of God. Whenever the church seeks its own interests and forgets God's plans, it is unfaithful to Jesus. Whenever Christians put their own interests ahead of those of the poorest, they are unfaithful to Jesus.

The second temptation takes place in the temple. The tempter invites Jesus to come down from on high like a glorious Messiah making a triumphal entry into the holy city. God's protection is assured. His angels will guard him. Jesus reacts quickly: «*Do not put the Lord your God to the test*». He will not be a triumphant Messiah. He will not put God at the service of his own glory. He will not perform «signs» in the heavens. His only signs will be to cure the sick.

Whenever the church puts God at the service of its own glory and descends from on high to show its own dignity, it is unfaithful to Jesus. When the followers of Christ want to be well-to-do instead of doing good, they are unfaithful to Jesus.

The third temptation takes place on a very high mountain. From there you can survey all the kingdoms of the world. All are under the control of Satan, who makes Jesus an astounding offer on one condition: «*if you will bow down and worship me*». Jesus reacts violently: «*Away from me, Satan! For it is written: "Worship the Lord your God, and serve him only"*». God does not send him to dominate the world like the Emperor of Rome, but to serve those who are oppressed. He will not be a dominating Messiah, but one who serves. God does not impose his kingdom on the world with the use of power, but offers it to humanity with love.

The church must banish all temptations of power, glory and domination by shouting with Jesus, «*Away from me, Satan!*» Worldly power is a diabolical scheme. When we Christians seek it, we are unfaithful to Christ.

2

Listen Only to Jesus

MATTHEW 17: 1-9

SECOND SUNDAY OF LENT

«After six days Jesus took with him Peter, James and John the brother of James, and led them up a high mountain by themselves. There he was transfigured before them. His face shone like the sun, and his clothes became as white as the light. Just then there appeared before them Moses and Elijah, talking with Jesus. Peter said to Jesus, "Lord, it is good for us to be here. If you wish, I will put up three shelters —one for you, one for Moses and one for Elijah". While he was still speaking, a bright cloud enveloped them, and a voice from the cloud said, "This is my Son, whom I love; with him I am well pleased. Listen to him!" When the disciples heard this, they fell facedown to the ground, terrified. But Jesus came and touched them. "Get up", he said. "Don't be afraid". When they looked up, they saw no one except Jesus. As they were coming down the mountain, Jesus instructed them, "Don't tell anyone what you have seen, until the Son of Man has been raised from the dead"».

Jesus takes with him his closest disciples and leads them to a high mountain. It is not the mountain to which the tempter took him to offer him the power and glory of all the kingdoms of the world. It is the mountain on which his closest disciples are going to discover the path leading to the glory of the resurrection.

The transfigured face of Jesus shines like the sun and shows them where his true glory comes from. It does not come from the devil but from God his Father. It is not acquired by the diabolical ways of worldly power, but by the patient way of hidden service, suffering and crucifixion. Moses and Elijah appear next to Jesus. Their faces do not shine, but look subdued. They do not begin to instruct the disciples, but instead they converse with Jesus. The law and the prophets look to and are subordinate to him.

Peter, however, fails to sense the uniqueness of Jesus: «*If you wish, I will put up three shelters —one for you, one for Moses and one for Elijah*». He puts Jesus on the same plane as Moses and Elijah. Each one gets a shelter. He does not understand that you cannot equate Jesus with anyone. God himself silences Peter. «*He was still speaking*» when between light and shadows they hear a mysterious voice: «*This is my Son, whom I love*», the one with the face glorified by the resurrection. «*Listen to him*», and nobody else. My Son is the only lawgiver, teacher and prophet. Do not confuse him with anyone else.

The disciples fall facedown on the ground «*full of terror*». They are afraid «*to listen only to Jesus*» and to follow his humble way of serving the Kingdom up to the cross. It is Jesus himself who frees them from their fears. He came to them as only he knew how to. He touched them as he touched the sick, and he said to them, «*Get up, do not be afraid*» to listen to me and to follow only me.

Even today we Christians fear to listen only to Jesus. We do not dare to place him at the center of our lives and our communities. We do not let him be the only and decisive Word. It is the same Jesus who can free us from so many fears, cowardice, and ambiguities, if we will let him come to us and touch us.

3
A More Human Dialogue

JOHN 4:5-42

THIRD SUNDAY OF LENT

«*So he came to a town in Samaria called Sychar, near the plot of ground Jacob had given to his son Joseph. Jacob's well was there, and Jesus, tired as he was from the journey, sat down by the well. It was about the sixth hour. When a Samaritan woman came to draw water, Jesus said to her, "Will you give me a drink?" (His disciples had gone into the town to buy food.) The Samaritan woman said to him, "You are a Jew and I am a Samaritan woman. How can you ask me for a drink?" (For Jews do not associate with Samaritans). Jesus answered her, "If you knew the gift of God and who it is that asks you for a drink, you would have asked him and he would have given you living water". "Sir", the woman said, "you have nothing to draw with and the well is deep. Where can you get this living water? Are you greater than our father Jacob, who gave us the well and drank from it himself, as did also his sons and his flocks and herds?" Jesus answered, "Everyone who drinks this water will be thirsty again, but whoever drinks the water I give him will never thirst. Indeed, the water I give him will become in him a spring of water welling up to eternal life". The woman said to him, "Sir, give me this water so that I won't get thirsty and have to keep coming here to draw water". He told her, "Go, call your husband and come back". "I have no husband", she replied. Jesus said to her, "You are right when you say you have no husband. The fact is, you have had five husbands, and the man you now have is not your husband. What you have just said is quite true". "Sir", the woman said, "I can see that you are a prophet. Our fathers worshiped on this mountain, but you Jews claim that the place where we must worship is in Jerusalem". Jesus declared, "Believe me, woman, a time is coming when you will worship*

Lent

53

the Father neither on this mountain nor in Jerusalem. You Samaritans worship what you do not know; we worship what we do know, for salvation is from the Jews. Yet a time is coming and has now come when the true worshipers will worship the Father in spirit and truth, for they are the kind of worshipers the Father seeks. God is spirit, and his worshipers must worship in spirit and in truth". The woman said, "I know that the Messiah (called Christ) is coming. When he comes, he will explain everything to us". Then Jesus declared, "I who speak to you am he"».

The scene is enchanting. Jesus reaches the small village of Sychar. He is tired from walking all the way. His life is a continual walking to and visiting of the towns, announcing that better world which God wants for all people. He needs to rest and he sits down at the well of Jacob.

Soon an unknown nameless woman arrives at the well. She is a Samaritan woman and comes to quench her thirst at the spring in the well. Quite spontaneously Jesus begins a conversation with her: «*Will you give me a drink?*»

How do you dare to come into contact with someone who belongs to an unclean and contemptible people like the Samaritans? How is it you lower yourself to ask for water from an unknown woman? That goes against everything imaginable in Israel. Jesus presents himself as someone in need. He needs to drink and seeks help and a welcome from the heart of that woman. There is a language we all understand because we all know what it is to feel tired or lonely, to thirst for happiness, to feel fear or sadness or be seriously ill. Our basic needs unite us and bring us to help each other, setting aside our differences. The woman is surprised that Jesus does not speak to her with the air of superiority proper to Jews in front of Samaritans, or with the arrogance of men towards women.

A new relationship has developed between Jesus and the woman. It is a more human one and it rings true. Jesus tells her of his deep desire: «*If you knew the gift of God*», if you knew that God is a gift, that he offers himself to all as love that saves. But the woman has not known unconditional love. Water has to be drawn from the well with hard labor. One after the other the love of her husbands has grown cold.

When the woman hears Jesus speak of water that quenches thirst forever, of an inner spring that wells up into life-giving fruitfulness and eternal life, a desire is awakened in her for the fullness of life that is in all of us: *«Sir, give me this water».* We can speak with anyone about God if we see ourselves as in need, if we share our thirst for happiness and overcome our differences, if prophets and religious leaders ask women for a drink, if we all together discover that God is love and only love.

4

Jesus Is for the Excluded

JOHN 9: 1-41

FOURTH SUNDAY OF LENT

> *«As he went along, he saw a man blind from birth. His disciples asked him, "Rabbi, who sinned, this man or his parents, that he was born blind?" "Neither this man nor his parents sinned", said Jesus, "but this happened so that the work of God might be displayed in his life. As long as it is day, we must do the work of him who sent me. Night is coming, when no one can work. While I am in the world, I am the light of the world". Having said this, he spit on the ground, made some mud with the saliva, and put it on the man's eyes. "Go", he told him, "wash in the Pool of Siloam" (this word means Sent). So the man went and washed, and came home seeing.*
>
> *His neighbors and those who had formerly seen him begging asked, "Isn't this the same man who used to sit and beg?" Some claimed that he was. Others said, "No, he only looks like him". But he himself insisted, "I am the man". "How then were*

your eyes opened?" they demanded. He replied, "The man they call Jesus made some mud and put it on my eyes. He told me to go to Siloam and wash. So I went and washed, and then I could see". "Where is this man?" they asked him. "I don't know", he said.

They brought to the Pharisees the man who had been blind. Now the day on which Jesus had made the mud and opened the man's eyes was a Sabbath. Therefore the Pharisees also asked him how he had received his sight. "He put mud on my eyes", the man replied, "and I washed, and now I see". Some of the Pharisees said, "This man is not from God, for he does not keep the Sabbath". But others asked, "How can a sinner do such miraculous signs?" So they were divided.

Finally they turned again to the blind man, "What have you to say about him? It was your eyes he opened". The man replied, "He is a prophet". The Jews still did not believe that he had been blind and had received his sight until they sent for the man's parents. "Is this your son?" they asked. "Is this the one you say was born blind? How is it that now he can see?" "We know he is our son", the parents answered, "and we know he was born blind. But how he can see now, or who opened his eyes, we don't know. Ask him. He is of age; he will speak for himself".

His parents said this because they were afraid of the Jews, for already the Jews had decided that anyone who acknowledged that Jesus was the Christ would be put out of the synagogue. That was why his parents said, "He is of age; ask him". A second time they summoned the man who had been blind. "Give glory to God", they said. "We know this man is a sinner". He replied, "Whether he is a sinner or not, I don't know. One thing I do know. I was blind but now I see!" Then they asked him, "What did he do to you? How did he open your eyes?" He answered, "I have told you already and you did not listen. Why do you want to hear it again? Do you want to become his disciples, too?"

Then they hurled insults at him and said, "You are this fellow's disciple! We are disciples of Moses! We know that God spoke to Moses, but as for this fellow, we don't even know where he comes from". The man answered, "Now that is remarkable!

You don't know where he comes from, yet he opened my eyes. We know that God does not listen to sinners. He listens to the godly man who does his will. Nobody has ever heard of opening the eyes of a man born blind. If this man were not from God, he could do nothing". To this they replied, "You were steeped in sin at birth; how dare you lecture us!" And they threw him out.

Jesus heard that they had thrown him out, and when he found him, he said, "Do you believe in the Son of Man?" "Who is he, sir?" the man asked. "Tell me so that I may believe in him". Jesus said, "You have now seen him; in fact, he is the one speaking with you". Then the man said, "Lord, I believe", and he worshiped him.

Jesus said, "For judgment I have come into this world, so that the blind will see and those who see will become blind". Some Pharisees who were with him heard him say this and asked, "What? Are we blind too?" Jesus said, "If you were blind, you would not be guilty of sin; but now that you claim you can see, your guilt remains".

The man is blind from birth. He does not know what light is. He has never known it. Neither he nor his parents are to blame. But there he is sitting, begging alms. It is his fate to live in darkness.

One day as Jesus passes by that way he sees the blind man. The evangelist says that Jesus is nothing less than the «light of the world». Perhaps he recalled the words of the ancient prophet Isaiah assuring all that one day someone would come to Israel who would cry out to the prisoners: «Come out!» and to those in darkness: «Come to the light!»

Jesus works on the eyes of the poor blind man with mud and saliva to pour into him his life. The cure is not automatic. The blind man too has to collaborate. He does what Jesus tells him to do: he washes his eyes, cleans them and begins to see. When the people ask him who cured him he does not know what to answer. It was a man called Jesus. He cannot say any more. Neither does he know where he is. He only knows that thanks to this man, he can now live life in a completely new way. This is what's important.

When the Pharisees and the religious experts harass him with questions, the man answers quite simply: «*I think he is a prophet*». He doesn't know much about Jesus, but obviously, someone who can open your eyes must come from God. The Pharisees get furious, insult him, and expel him from the religious community.

The reaction of Jesus is touching. When he learns that they had thrown the man out, he goes to look for him. That's the way Jesus is. We must never forget the one who comes to seek out men and women who feel they have been thrown out of religion. Jesus does not abandon those who seek and love him even though they have been excluded from their religious community.

It is a brief exchange: «*Do you believe in the Son of Man?*» The man is willing to believe. In his heart he is a believer, but he doesn't know anything more. «*Who is he, sir?*» *the man asked.* «*Tell me so that I may believe in him*». *Jesus said,* «*You have now seen him; in fact, he is the one speaking with you*». According to the evangelist this event took place in Jerusalem about the year 30 and continues to take place among us in the twenty-first century.

5

There Is Life in Their Graves

JOHN 11: 1-45

FIFTH SUNDAY OF LENT

«*Now a man named Lazarus was sick. He was from Bethany, the village of Mary and her sister Martha. This Mary, whose brother Lazarus now lay sick, was the same one who poured perfume on the Lord and wiped his feet with her hair. So the sisters sent word to Jesus, "Lord, the one you love is sick". When he* heard this, Jesus said, "This sickness will not end in death. No, it is for God's glory so that God's Son may be glorified through it".

Jesus loved Martha and her sister and Lazarus. Yet when he heard that Lazarus was sick, he stayed where he was two more days. Then he said to his disciples, "Let us go back to Judea". "But Rabbi", they said, "a short while ago the Jews tried to stone you, and yet you are going back there?" Jesus answered, "Are there not twelve hours of daylight? A man who walks by day will not stumble, for he sees by this world's light. It is when he walks by night that he stumbles, for he has no light".

After he had said this, he went on to tell them, "Our friend Lazarus has fallen asleep; but I am going there to wake him up". His disciples replied, "Lord, if he sleeps, he will get better". Jesus had been speaking of his death, but his disciples thought he meant natural sleep. So then he told them plainly, "Lazarus is dead, and for your sake I am glad I was not there, so that you may believe. But let us go to him". Then Thomas (called Didymus) said to the rest of the disciples, "Let us also go, that we may die with him".

On his arrival, Jesus found that Lazarus had already been in the tomb for four days. Bethany was less than two miles from Jerusalem, and many Jews had come to Martha and Mary to comfort them in the loss of their brother. When Martha heard that Jesus was coming, she went out to meet him, but Mary stayed at home.

"Lord", Martha said to Jesus, "if you had been here, my brother would not have died. But I know that even now God will give you whatever you ask". Jesus said to her, "Your brother will rise again". Martha answered, "I know he will rise again in the resurrection at the last day". Jesus said to her, "I am the resurrection and the life. He who believes in me will live, even though he dies; and whoever lives and believes in me will never die. Do you believe this?" "Yes, Lord", she told him, "I believe that you are the Christ, the Son of God, who was to come into the world". And after she had said this, she went back and called her sister Mary aside. "The Teacher is here", she said, "and is asking for you". When Mary heard this, she got up quickly and went to him.

Now Jesus had not yet entered the village, but was still at the place where Martha had met him. When the Jews who had been with Mary in the house, comforting her, noticed how quickly she got up and went out, they followed her, supposing she was going to the tomb to mourn there. When Mary reached the place where Jesus was and saw him, she fell at his feet and said, "Lord, if you had been here, my brother would not have died". When Jesus saw her weeping, and the Jews who had come along with her also weeping, he was deeply moved in spirit and troubled.

"Where have you laid him?" he asked. "Come and see, Lord", they replied. Jesus wept. Then the Jews said, "See how he loved him!" But some of them said, "Could not he who opened the eyes of the blind man have kept this man from dying?" Jesus, once more deeply moved, came to the tomb. It was a cave with a stone laid across the entrance. "Take away the stone", he said. "But, Lord", said Martha, the sister of the dead man, "by this time there is a bad odor, for he has been there four days". Then Jesus said, "Did I not tell you that if you believed, you would see the glory of God?"

So they took away the stone. Then Jesus looked up and said, "Father, I thank you that you have heard me. I knew that you always hear me, but I said this for the benefit of the people standing here, that they may believe that you sent me". When he had said this, Jesus called in a loud voice, "Lazarus, come out!" The dead man came out, his hands and feet wrapped with strips of linen, and a cloth around his face. Jesus said to them, "Take off the grave clothes and let him go"».

The final farewell to a dearly loved one plunges us inevitably into sorrow, leaving us feeling impotent and without purpose. It is as if the whole of our lives has been destroyed. No words or explanations can console us. What is there to hope in?

John's account is not only intended to narrate the resurrection of Lazarus, but beyond that to awaken our faith, so that we not only believe in the resurrection as a distant event that will take place at the end of the world, but also that we may see that God is already here and now, infusing life into those we have buried.

Jesus arrives sobbing at the grave of his friend Lazarus. The evangelist says that it is closed with a stone. That stone blocks our way. We know nothing about our dead friends. A stone separates the world of the living from that of the dead. We can only wait for the last day to see if something happens.

This is the Jewish faith of Martha: «*I know that my brother will rise in the resurrection on the last day*». That is not enough for Jesus. «*Take away the stone*». Let us see what has happened to the man you have buried. Martha pleads with Jesus to be realistic. The body of the dead man is decomposing and there's a bad odor. Jesus answers her: «*If you believe, you will see the glory of God*». If the faith of Martha is awakened, she will be able to see that God is giving life to her brother.

«*Take away the stone*». And Jesus raises his eyes on high inviting all to raise their eyes to God before they penetrate with faith the mystery of death. He has stopped sobbing. He gives thanks to the Father because he always hears him. What he wants is that those about him believe that he is the one sent by the Father to bring new hope into the world.

Then he cries out in a powerful voice: «*Lazarus, come forth*». He wants him to come out to show all of them that he is alive. The scene is shocking. Lazarus has his hands and his feet bound in linen strips and his face wrapped in a cloth. He has the signs and bonds of death. However, the dead man comes out by himself. He is alive.

This is the faith of those who believe in Jesus: those whom we bury and abandon in death still live. God has not abandoned them. Take away the stone with faith. Our dead are alive.

6

Take Up the Cross

∽

62

«Then one of the Twelve —the one called Judas Iscariot— went to the chief priests and asked, "What are you willing to give me if I hand him over to you?" So they counted out for him thirty silver coins. From then on Judas watched for an opportunity to hand him over.

On the first day of the Feast of Unleavened Bread, the disciples came to Jesus and asked, "Where do you want us to make preparations for you to eat the Passover?" He replied, "Go into the city to a certain man and tell him, 'The Teacher says: My appointed time is near. I am going to celebrate the Passover with my disciples at your house'". So the disciples did as Jesus had directed them and prepared the Passover.

When evening came, Jesus was reclining at the table with the Twelve. And while they were eating, he said, "I tell you the truth, one of you will betray me". They were very sad and began to say to him one after the other, "Surely not I, Lord?" Jesus replied, "The one who has dipped his hand into the bowl with me will betray me. The Son of Man will go just as it is written about him. But woe to that man who betrays the Son of Man! It would be better for him if he had not been born". Then Judas, the one who would betray him, said, "Surely not I, Rabbi?" Jesus answered, "Yes, it is you". While they were eating, Jesus took bread, gave thanks and broke it, and gave it to his disciples, saying, "Take and eat; this is my body". Then he took the cup, gave thanks and offered it to them, saying, "Drink from it, all of you".

"What do you think?" "He is worthy of death", they answered».

What makes us Christian is to follow Jesus. That's all. This following of Jesus is not theoretical or abstract. It means following in his footsteps, committing ourselves to humanizing life and so contributing little by little to making a reality of his project of a world in which God and his justice reign. This means that we, the followers of Jesus, are sent to bring truth where there is deceit and lies, justice where there is injustice and cruelty to the weakest, and to bring back compassion where there is indifference and passivity at the sight of those who suffer. This entails building communities that unite on the basis of the project of Jesus while living his spirit and attitudes.

Following Jesus sooner or later brings with it conflicts, problems and suffering. One must be ready to face reactions and resistance from those who for one reason or another do not want a more human world such as the kind that God wants as revealed by Jesus. They want something else.

The Gospels have preserved a realistic call of Jesus to his followers. The shock his metaphorical image carries with it can only come from him: *«If someone wants to come after me… let him take up his cross and follow me»*. Jesus does not deceive us. If we really follow him, we will have to suffer his fate. We will end up like him. That will be the final proof that we have been faithful in following him.

To follow Jesus is an all-consuming task. It is difficult to imagine a life more noble or dignified. But there's a price to be paid. To follow Jesus it is important to «do»: to make the world more just; to create a Church more faithful to the Gospels. Yet it is as important or more so to «suffer» in bringing about a more just world, to suffer building a church more faithful to the Gospels.

At the end of his life the theologian, Karl Rahner wrote: «I believe that being Christian is the most simple task; the most simple and at the same time it is the heavy "light burden" of which the Gospels speak. When one lifts it, it lifts you, and the longer you live, the heavier and lighter it becomes. At the end only the mystery remains, but it is the mystery of Jesus».

Part four

Easter

The Scars of the Risen One

JOHN 20:1-9

EASTER SUNDAY

«*Early on the first day of the week, while it was still dark, Mary Magdalene went to the tomb and saw that the stone had been removed from the entrance. So she came running to Simon Peter and the other disciple, the one Jesus loved, and said, "They have taken the Lord out of the tomb, and we don't know where they have put him!"*

So Peter and the other disciple started for the tomb. Both were running, but the other disciple outran Peter and reached the tomb first. He bent over and looked in at the strips of linen lying there but did not go in. Then Simon Peter, who was behind him, arrived and went into the tomb. He saw the strips of linen lying there, as well as the burial cloth that had been around Jesus' head. The cloth was folded up by itself, separate from the linen.

Finally the other disciple, who had reached the tomb first, also went inside. He saw and believed. (They still did not understand from Scripture that Jesus had to rise from the dead)».

«You killed him, but God raised him from the dead». This is what the disciples preach with faith in the streets of Jerusalem within a few days of the resurrection of Jesus. For them the resurrection is the answer of God to the unjust and criminal act of those who wanted to silence his voice and put an end to his project of a more just world. We must never forget this. At the heart of our faith there is a crucified man whom God has proven right. At the very heart of the church there is a victim to whom God has done justice. A crucified life, inspired by and lived in the spirit of Jesus, will not end in failure but in resurrection.

This changes altogether the meaning of our efforts, pain, work, and suffering for a world that is more human and for a more just life for all. It is not a senseless venture to live with concern for those who suffer, to reach out to the most needy, to help the helpless; it means journeying to the mystery of a God who will resurrect our lives forever.

The little abuses we suffer, the injustices, rejection and misunderstandings are wounds that one day will become scars forever. We must learn to regard the scars of the risen one with greater faith. This is how our wounds will appear one day —like scars healed by God forever. This kind of faith will sustain us from within, and strengthen us to continue risking our lives. Slowly we have to learn not to complain so much, not to keep always lamenting the evil there is in the world and in the church, not to always feel we are the victims of the others. Why can we not live like Jesus saying: «*No one takes away my life. It is I who give it*».

To follow the crucified one until we share in the resurrection with him is finally to learn to give our lives, our time, our efforts, and perhaps our health for the sake of love. We will not lack wounds, weariness and pain. This is the hope that will sustain us: «*He will wipe every tear from their eyes. There will be no more death or mourning or crying or pain, for the old order of things has passed away*».

2

Do Not Hide the Risen One

JOHN 20: 19-31

SECOND SUNDAY OF EASTER

«*On the evening of that first day of the week, when the disciples were together, with the doors locked for fear of the Jews, Jesus came and stood among them and said, "Peace be with you!" After he said this, he showed them his hands and side. The dis-*

ciples were overjoyed when they saw the Lord. Again Jesus said, "Peace be with you! As the Father has sent me, I am sending you". And with that he breathed on them and said, "Receive the Holy Spirit. If you forgive anyone his sins, they are forgiven; if you do not forgive them, they are not forgiven".

Now Thomas (called Didymus), one of the Twelve, was not with the disciples when Jesus came. So the other disciples told him, "We have seen the Lord!" But he said to them, "Unless I see the nail marks in his hands and put my finger where the nails were, and put my hand into his side, I will not believe it". A week later his disciples were in the house again, and Thomas was with them. Though the doors were locked, Jesus came and stood among them and said, "Peace be with you!" Then he said to Thomas, "Put your finger here; see my hands. Reach out your hand and put it into my side. Stop doubting and believe". Thomas said to him, "My Lord and my God!"

Then Jesus told him, "Because you have seen me, you have believed, blessed are those who have not seen and yet have believed". Jesus did many other miraculous signs in the presence of his disciples, which are not recorded in this book. But these are written that you may believe that Jesus is the Christ, the Son of God, and that by believing you may have life in his name».

Mary Magdalene has shared her experience with the disciples and has declared that Jesus is alive, but they remain closed up in a house with the doors locked for fear of the Jews. The announcement of the resurrection does not dispel their fears. It does not have the power to awaken joy in them. The evangelist evokes in a few words their helplessness in the midst of a hostile environment. Night is falling. Their fear prompts them to keep all the doors safely closed. They only want to be safe. It is their only concern. Nobody thinks of the mission they've received from Jesus.

It is not enough to know that the Lord has risen. It is not enough to hear the Easter message. Those disciples miss the most important thing: the experience of feeling Jesus alive in their midst. It is only when Jesus is the center of the community that he becomes the source of life, of joy and of peace for the believers.

The disciples are filled with joy on seeing the Lord. This is what always happens. There is joy in a Christian community when it is possible to «see» Jesus alive in the midst of all. Our communities will not overcome their fears, nor will they feel the joy of the faith, or know the peace that only Christ can give, as long as Jesus does not occupy the center of our meetings, gatherings and assemblies, and as long as he is overshadowed by others.

Sometimes it is we ourselves who make him disappear. We meet in his name, but Jesus is absent from our hearts. We exchange the sign of peace of the Lord, but it is all reduced to a greeting among us. The gospel is read and we proclaim it is the «word of the Lord», but sometimes we only listen to what the preacher says.

In the church we always talk about Jesus. In theory there is nothing more important for us. Jesus is constantly preached, taught, and celebrated, but in the hearts of not a few Christians there is a void; it is as if Jesus were absent, hidden by traditions, customs, and routine practices that consign him to the background. Perhaps our main task today is to place Jesus at the heart of our communities —a Jesus we know, love and follow with passion. It is when we commit ourselves in this way that the parish and the diocese are at their best.

3
Two Key Experiences

LUKE 24: 13-35

THIRD SUNDAY OF EASTER

«Now that same day two of them were going to a village called Emmaus, about seven miles from Jerusalem. They were talking with each other about everything that had happened. As they talked and discussed these things with each other, Jesus himself came up and walked along with them; but they were kept from recognizing him.

He asked them, "What are you discussing together as you walk along?" They stood still, their faces downcast. One of them, named Cleopas, asked him, "Are you only a visitor to Jerusalem and do not know the things that have happened there in these days?"

"What things?" he asked. "About Jesus of Nazareth", they replied. "He was a prophet, powerful in word and deed before God and all the people. The chief priests and our rulers handed him over to be sentenced to death, and they crucified him; but we had hoped that he was the one who was going to redeem Israel. And what is more, it is the third day since all this took place. In addition, some of our women amazed us. They went to the tomb early this morning but didn't find his body. They came and told us that they had seen a vision of angels, who said he was alive. Then some of our companions went to the tomb and found it just as the women had said, but him they did not see".

He said to them, "How foolish you are, and how slow of heart to believe all that the prophets have spoken! Did not the Christ have to suffer these things and then enter his glory?" And beginning with Moses and all the Prophets, he explained to them what was said in all the Scriptures concerning himself.

As they approached the village to which they were going, Jesus acted as if he were going farther. But they urged him strongly,

"Stay with us, for it is nearly evening; the day is almost over". So he went in to stay with them.

When he was at the table with them, he took bread, gave thanks, broke it and began to give it to them. Then their eyes were opened and they recognized him, and he disappeared from their sight. They asked each other, "Were not our hearts burning within us while he talked with us on the road and opened the Scriptures to us?"

They got up and returned at once to Jerusalem. There they found the Eleven and those with them, assembled together and saying, "It is true! The Lord has risen and has appeared to Simon". Then the two told what had happened on the way, and how Jesus was recognized by them when he broke the bread».

Over the years a very real problem arose quite naturally in the Christian community. Peter, Mary Magdalene and the other disciples had had very special experiences of meeting Jesus alive after his death. Through these experiences they were led to believe in the Risen Jesus. But could those who joined the group of followers later also awaken and nourish that same faith?

We have the same problem today. We have not had the same experiences as the earliest disciples had. What experiences can we depend on? This is the problem the story of the disciples of Emmaus addresses.

The two disciples walk back sad and desolate to their homes. They have lost their faith in Jesus. They do not hope for anything from him. It's all been an illusion. Jesus, who has been following them without being noticed, catches up with them and walks with them. Luke explains the situation: «*But their eyes were unable to recognize him*». What can they do to be able to recognize his presence by their side?

The important thing is that these disciples do not forget Jesus; they «talk and discuss» about him; they remember his words and his deeds as those of a great prophet; they let that stranger keep clarifying all that had happened. Their eyes are not opened immediately, but their hearts begin to burn.

What we most of all need in our communities is to remember Jesus, to understand deeply his message and his actions, to meditate on his crucifixion. If, at some point, Jesus moves us deeply, his words reach deep within us, and our hearts begin to burn, it is a sign that our faith has begun to awaken.

This is not enough, however. Luke understands that the experience of the Eucharist is also necessary. Even though they do not yet know who he is, the two travelers feel the need for Jesus. His company does them good. They don't want him to leave them. «*Stay with us*». Luke stresses with joy: «*He went in to stay with them*». During supper their eyes were opened.

These are two key experiences: to feel our hearts burning on hearing his message, on learning about his deeds and his whole life; and when we celebrate the Eucharist to feel that he nourishes us, strengthens us and comforts us. In this way faith in the Risen Christ grows.

4

Through the Right Door

JOHN 10: 1-10

FOURTH SUNDAY OF EASTER

«*"I tell you the truth, the man who does not enter the sheep pen by the gate, but climbs in by some other way, is a thief and a robber. The man who enters by the gate is the shepherd of his sheep. The watchman opens the gate for him, and the sheep listen to his voice. He calls his own sheep by name and leads them out. When he has brought out all his own, he goes on ahead of them, and his sheep follow him because they know his voice.*

"But they will never follow a stranger; in fact, they will run away from him because they do not recognize a stranger's voice". Jesus used this figure of speech, but they did not understand what he was telling them. Therefore Jesus said again, "I tell you the truth, I am the gate for the sheep. All who ever came before

me were thieves and robbers, but the sheep did not listen to them. I am the gate; whoever enters through me will be saved. He will come in and go out, and find pasture. The thief comes only to steal and kill and destroy; I have come that they may have life, and have it to the full"».

The Gospel of John presents us with original and beautiful images of Jesus. He wants his readers to discover that only Jesus can fully meet the most fundamental needs of the human person. «He is *the bread of life*». Whoever is nourished by him will not hunger. He is «*the light of the world*». Whoever follows him will not walk in darkness. He is the «*good shepherd*». Whoever listens to his voice will find life.

Among these images there is one, ordinary and almost forgotten, which nevertheless has a deep significance: «*I am the door*». That is what Jesus is, an open door. Whoever follows him crosses a threshold that leads to a new world: a new way of understanding and living life.

The evangelist explains it with three details. First, «*Whoever enters through me will be saved*». There are many options in life. Not all lead to success or guarantee a full life. Whoever has some understanding of Jesus and tries to follow him enters through the right door. He will not lose his life; he will save it.

The evangelist then says something more. Whoever enters through Jesus, can «*come and go*». He is free to move around. He enters a space where he can be free, for he is guided only by the Spirit of Jesus. It is not the land of anarchy or licentious freedom. He «comes and goes», always passing through that door that is Jesus and he follows his footsteps.

The evangelist further adds another detail: whoever enters through that door that is Jesus will «*find pasture*». He will not hunger or thirst. He will find solid and abundant nourishment to live on. Christ is the door through which we Christians must enter today if we wish to revive our identity. A Christianity made up of Christians who relate to a badly known, vaguely remembered Jesus, occasionally acknowledged in a theoretical way, a dumb Jesus with nothing to say to today's world, a Jesus who does not touch our hearts, is Christianity without a future.

Only Christ can lead us to a new level of Christian life, more firmly grounded in, motivated and nourished by the gospel. Each one of us can, in the coming years, contribute to a church in which Jesus is experienced and lived in a more zealous and passionate way. We can create a church more like the one Jesus wanted.

5
We Know the Way

JOHN 14: 1-12

FIFTH SUNDAY OF EASTER

« *"Do not let your hearts be troubled. Trust in God; trust also in me. In my Father's house are many rooms; if it were not so, I would have told you. I am going there to prepare a place for you. And if I go and prepare a place for you, I will come back and take you to be with me that you also may be where I am. You know the way to the place where I am going".*

Thomas said to him, "Lord, we don't know where you are going, so how can we know the way?" Jesus answered, "I am the way and the truth and the life. No one comes to the Father except through me. If you really knew me, you would know my Father as well. From now on, you do know him and have seen him". Philip said, "Lord, show us the Father and that will be enough for us". Jesus answered: "Don't you know me, Philip, even after I have been among you such a long time? Anyone who has seen me has seen the Father. How can you say, 'Show us the Father'?

"Don't you believe that I am in the Father, and that the Father is in me? The words I say to you are not just my own. Rather, it is the Father, living in me, who is doing his work. Believe me

when I say that I am in the Father and the Father is in me; or at least believe on the evidence of the miracles themselves. I tell you the truth, anyone who has faith in me will do what I have been doing. He will do even greater things than these, because I am going to the Father"».

They had lived with Jesus only two years and some months, but with him they had learned to live with faith. Now, on being separated, Jesus wants to have this strongly imprinted in their hearts: «*Do not let your hearts be troubled. Trust in God; trust also in me*». It is his great desire.

Then Jesus begins to tell them of things that no one on earth had ever spoken of before: «*I am going to prepare a place for you in the house of my Father*». Death will not destroy the bonds of our love. One day we will be together. «*You know the way to the place where I am going*». The disciples are bewildered by what they heard. How can they not be afraid? Jesus himself who had inspired in them so much trust would soon be snatched away so unjustly and cruelly. In the end, in whom can we ultimately place our hope?

Thomas intervenes to bring them down to reality. «*Lord, we don't know where you are going, so how can we know the way?*» Jesus responds without hesitation: «*I am the way that leads to the Father*». He is the way that leads from now on to the experience of God as Father. The others are not ways. They are diversions that lead us away from the truth and life. What matters most is to follow in the footsteps of Jesus until we reach the Father. Philip sensed that Jesus was not talking about just any religious experience. It is not enough to believe in an all-powerful God to experience his goodness, or one who is too great and distant to experience his mercy. What Jesus wants to instill in them is different. So he says: «*Show us the Father and that will be enough for us*».

The response of Jesus is unexpected and magnificent: «*Whoever has seen me, has seen the Father*». The life of Jesus: his goodness, his freedom to do good, his forgiveness, his love for the «least» —these all make the Father visible and credible. His life reveals to us that in the depths of reality there resides the ultimate mystery of goodness and love. He calls it «Father».

Christians are sustained by these two sayings of Jesus: «*Do not be afraid because I go to prepare a place for you in the house of my Father*», and «*Whoever sees me, sees the Father*». Whenever we dare to live up to something of the goodness, the freedom and the compassion that Jesus brought into the world, we will make more credible a God who is a Father and the ultimate source of our hope.

6

Living in the Truth of Jesus

> «*"If you love me, you will obey what I command. And I will ask the Father, and he will give you another Counselor to be with you forever —the Spirit of truth. The world cannot accept him, because it neither sees him nor knows him. But you know him, for he lives with you and will be in you. I will not leave you as orphans; I will come to you. Before long, the world will not see me anymore, but you will see me. Because I live, you also will live.*
>
> *"On that day you will realize that I am in my Father, and you are in me, and I am in you. Whoever has my commands and obeys them, he is the one who loves me. He who loves me will be loved by my Father, and I too will love him and show myself to him"*».

There is no experience in life as mysterious and sacred as the departure of a loved one who leaves us for a place beyond death. And so the Gospel of John tries to draw up his last will in the final farewell of Jesus. What will they do now without Jesus?

One thing is very clear for the evangelist. The world will not be able to «see» or «know» the truth hidden in Jesus. For most people Jesus will have passed through this world as if nothing had taken place. He will leave no vestige in their lives. They will need new eyes. Only those who love him will be able to experience Jesus as alive and life giving.

Jesus is the only person who deserves to be loved unconditionally. Whoever loves him in this way cannot think of him as someone belonging to the past. His life is not a memory. Whoever loves Jesus remembers his teachings, obeys his commandments, and keeps assimilating the life of Jesus.

It is not easy to speak of this experience. The evangelist calls it the Spirit of truth. That is true precisely because Jesus becomes a force and a light that makes us live in the truth. To accept Jesus in our lives leads us to the truth, no matter in what situation we may find ourselves in life.

We must not confuse this «Spirit of truth» with any doctrine. It is not to be found in the studies of theologians and not in official documents of church teachings. According to the promise of Jesus, «*he lives in us and is in us*». We listen to Jesus in our hearts, and he shines in the lives of those who follow his footsteps, with humility, confidence, and faith.

The evangelist identifies the Spirit as «Defender», because now that Jesus is no longer physically with us he defends us from what can separate us from him. This Spirit is always with us. No one can kill him as they did Jesus. He will always be alive in the world. If we accept him in our lives we will not remain orphans or forsaken.

Perhaps the conversion we Christians are most in need of today is to move from a verbal, routine and unreal attachment to Jesus to an experience of a life rooted in the «Spirit of truth».

Make Disciples of Jesus

MATTHEW 28:16-20

THE ASCENSION OF THE LORD

> «*Then the eleven disciples went to Galilee, to the mountain where Jesus had told them to go. When they saw him, they worshiped him; but some doubted. Then Jesus came to them and said, "All authority in heaven and on earth has been given to me. Therefore go and make disciples of all nations, baptizing them in the name of the Father and of the Son and of the Holy Spirit, and teaching them to obey everything I have commanded you. And surely I am with you always, to the very end of the age"*».

Matthew describes the departure of Jesus by delineating the bold outlines of what must guide the disciples forever, the characteristics that must mark the church in order to fulfill his mission.

Galilee is the starting point. Jesus summons them there. His resurrection should not lead them to forget what they experienced with him in Galilee. There he spoke to them of God in heart-warming parables. There they have seen him relieving suffering, bringing the forgiveness of God, and welcoming the most forsaken. That is exactly what they must continue to pass on.

There are believers among the disciples, and there are those who hesitate. The narrator is a realist. The disciples «prostrate themselves». Doubtless they want to believe, but there are some who doubt and are undecided. Perhaps they are frightened and cannot grasp the meaning of it all. Matthew knows how weak the faith of the Christian communities is. If they could not trust in Jesus, their faith would soon be extinguished.

Jesus draws near and comes into contact with them. He has the strength and the power they lack. He, the Risen one, has received the authority of the Son of God from the Father with «full authority in heaven and on earth». If they trust in him they will not hesitate. Jesus shows them in very precise terms what their mission is to be. It is not exactly «to teach doctrine». It is not only to proclaim that he has risen. No doubt the disciples of Jesus will have to take care of various aspects: to witness to the Risen one, to proclaim the Good News, to establish communities; but everything must finally be directed to one objective: to «make disciples» of Jesus.

This is our mission: to make followers of Jesus who know his message, identify with his project, learn to live like him, and reproduce his presence in the world. Such fundamental activities as baptism, commitment to belong to Jesus, and the teaching «of all that he has commanded», are ways in which to learn to become his disciples. Jesus promises his presence and his constant help. His followers will not be alone or forsaken, even if they are few, not even if they are two or three.

This is what the Christian community is designed to be. The power of the Risen One fills everything with his Spirit. Everything is directed to learning and teaching to live like Jesus, strengthened by him. He remains alive in his communities. He continues with us and among us, healing, forgiving, welcoming, and thus humanizing life.

«*On the evening of that first day of the week, when the disciples were together, with the doors locked for fear of the Jews, Jesus came and stood among them and said, "Peace be with you!" After he said this, he showed them his hands and side. The disciples were overjoyed when they saw the Lord. Again Jesus said, "Peace be with you! As the Father has sent me, I am sending you". And with that he breathed on them and said, "Receive the Holy Spirit. If you forgive anyone his sins, they are forgiven; if you do not forgive them, they are not forgiven"*».

John has taken great care over the scene in which Jesus will entrust his mission to his disciples. He wants to make what is essential very clear. Jesus is in the midst of the community, filling them with his peace and his joy. But a mission awaits the disciples. Jesus has not brought them together only to enjoy his presence, but in order for them to make him present in the world.

Jesus «sends» them. He doesn't tell them concretely to whom they have to go, what they have to do, and how they have to act. «*As the Father has sent me, so I send you*». Their task is the same as that of Jesus. They have no other task than what Jesus has received from the Father. They have to be in the world what Jesus has been in it.

They have seen to whom he has reached out, how he has treated the helpless, how he has carried on his project of humanizing life, how he has sown deeds of liberation and forgiveness. The wounds in his hands and his side remind them of his total commitment. Jesus now sends them to reproduce his presence among the nations.

But he knows the weakness of his disciples. More than once he was surprised at their little faith. They need his Spirit to accomplish his mission. So he prepares to do something special for them. He does not impose his hands on them; neither does he bless them as he used to do with the sick and the little ones. Instead, «*He breathed on them and said: Receive the Holy Spirit*».

The action of Jesus has a power that we do not always know how to appreciate. According to biblical tradition, God formed Adam with clay and then breathed life-giving breath into him, and that clay became a living being, that is, the human being —a little clay into which the Spirit of God has been breathed. That will always be what the church is: clay breathed into by the Spirit of God.

Weak believers of little faith are Christians of clay, theologians of clay, bishops of clay, and communities of clay. Only the Spirit of Jesus makes us a living church. The sectors in which the Spirit is not received remain dead. They hurt all of us, because they prevent the living Jesus from being made present. Many people cannot see in us the peace, the joy and the life renewed by Christ. We must not baptize only with water, but we must impart the Spirit of Jesus. We must not only speak of love, but must love people as he loved them.

Part five

Ordinary Time

1

Let Us Be Baptized by the Spirit

SECOND SUNDAY OF ORDINARY TIME

«*The next day John saw Jesus coming toward him and said, "Look, the Lamb of God, who takes away the sin of the world! This is the one I meant when I said, 'A man who comes after me has surpassed me because he was before me'. I myself did not know him, but the reason I came baptizing with water was that he might be revealed to Israel".*

Then John gave this testimony: "I saw the Spirit come down from heaven as a dove and remain on him. I would not have known him, except that the one who sent me to baptize with water told me, 'The man on whom you see the Spirit come down and remain is he who will baptize with the Holy Spirit'. I have seen and I testify that this is the Son of God"».

The evangelists work to keep the baptism of Jesus and that of John apart. They are not to be confused. The baptism of Jesus does not consist in immersing followers in the waters of a river. Jesus immerses them in the Holy Spirit.

John's Gospel says clearly that Jesus has the fullness of the Spirit of God and, therefore, can give of that fullness to his followers. The extraordinary originality of Jesus is that Jesus is «the Son of God» who can «baptize with the Holy Spirit».

This baptism of Jesus is not a form of external bathing, as some may have known perhaps in the waters of the Jordan. His is an «internal bathing». The metaphor suggests that Jesus communicates His Spirit to penetrate, soak and transform the heart of the person.

The Holy Spirit is regarded by the evangelists as the «*Spirit of Life*». So, to accept being baptized by Jesus means accepting his Spirit as a source of new life. His Spirit can empower us through a vital relationship with him. He can raise us to a new level of Christian existence, to a new stage of Christianity that is more faithful to Jesus.

The Spirit of Jesus is the «*Spirit of Truth*». To accept being baptized by him is to put truth in our Christianity. It is not to allow ourselves to be misled by false assurances; to recover again and again our identity as followers of Jesus that can never be renounced; to give up ways that lead us astray from the gospel.

The Spirit of Jesus is the «*Spirit of Love*», able to free us from cowardice and the selfishness that makes us think only of our interests and our prosperity. To accept being baptized by him is to be open to a love that is inclusive, gratuitous and compassionate.

The Spirit of Jesus is the «*Spirit of Conversion*» to God. To accept being baptized by Jesus means to let ourselves be transformed by him slowly, learning to live by his criteria, his attitudes, his heart and his sensitivity to anything that dehumanizes the children of God.

The Spirit of Jesus is the «*Spirit of Renewal*». To accept being baptized by Jesus is to accept being drawn into his creative newness. He can awaken the best there is in the church and give it a new heart with a greater ability to be faithful to the gospel.

2

The Core Word of Jesus

MATTHEW 4: 12-23

THIRD SUNDAY OF ORDINARY TIME

> «*When Jesus heard that John had been put in prison, he returned to Galilee. Leaving Nazareth, he went and lived in Capernaum, which was by the lake in the area of Zebulun and Naphtali —to fulfill what was said through the prophet Isaiah: "Land of*

Zebulun and land of Naphtali, the way to the sea, along the Jordan, Galilee of the Gentiles —the people living in darkness have seen a great light; on those living in the land of the shadow of death a light has dawned". From that time on Jesus began to preach, "Repent, for the kingdom of heaven is near".

As Jesus was walking beside the Sea of Galilee, he saw two brothers, Simon called Peter and his brother Andrew. They were casting a net into the lake, for they were fishermen. "Come, follow me", Jesus said, "and I will make you fishers of men". At once they left their nets and followed him. Going on from there, he saw two other brothers, James son of Zebedee and his brother John. They were in a boat with their father Zebedee, preparing their nets. Jesus called them, and immediately they left the boat and their father and followed him. Jesus went throughout Galilee, teaching in their synagogues, preaching the good news of the kingdom, and healing every disease and sickness among the people».

The evangelist Matthew takes great care to set the scene in which Jesus will make his first public appearance. He turns off the voice of the Baptist and the new voice of Jesus begins to be heard. The dry and gloomy landscape of the desert disappears and the greenery and beauty of Galilee occupy the center. Jesus leaves Nazareth and moves to Capernaum to the shore of the lake. Everything suggests the appearance of new life.

Matthew reminds us that we are in the Galilee of the Gentiles. He knows that Jesus has preached in Jewish synagogues of those villages and has not moved among pagans. But Galilee is the crossroads, and Capernaum is a city open to the sea. From here salvation will spread to all the peoples.

The situation now is tragic. Inspired by a text from Isaiah, Matthew sees «*the people dwelling in darkness*». On the earth «*there are shadows of death*». Chaos, injustice, and evil reign. Life cannot flourish. Things are not as God wants them. The Father does not reign here. However, in the midst of darkness, the people will start seeing «*a great light*». In the shadows of death, «*a light begins to shine*». That's always what Jesus is, a great light shining in the world.

According to Matthew, Jesus began his preaching with the word «*Repent*». This is his first, basic word. This is the time for conversion. Open yourselves to the kingdom of God. Do not «*sit in darkness*» but «*walk in the light*».

Within the church there is a «*great light*». It is Jesus. In him God reveals himself to us. Do not eclipse him with your leading roles. Do not replace him with anything. Do not turn him into theoretical doctrines, unfeeling theology, or boring sermons. If the light of Jesus goes out, we will become the Christians Jesus feared so much we might be: «*the blind leading the blind*».

Therefore, even today the first word of Jesus that we must listen to in the church is «*Repent*». Retrieve our Christian identity. Go back to our roots. Help the church to move into a new phase of Christianity more faithful to Jesus. Live with a new consciousness of being followers of Jesus. Put ourselves at the service of God's kingdom. Pray for a new heart for the church.

3

The Beatitudes

MATTHEW 5:1-12A

FOURTH SUNDAY OF ORDINARY TIME

> «*Now when he saw the crowds, he went up on a mountainside and sat down. His disciples came to him, and he began to teach them, saying:*
>
> > *Blessed are the poor in spirit, for theirs is the kingdom of heaven.*
> > *Blessed are those who mourn, for they will be comforted.*
> > *Blessed are the meek, for they will inherit the earth.*

Blessed are those who hunger and thirst for righteousness, for they will be filled.

Blessed are the merciful, for they will be shown mercy.

Blessed are the pure in heart, for they will see God.

Blessed are the peacemakers, for they will be called sons of God.

Blessed are those who are persecuted because of righteousness, for theirs is the kingdom of heaven.

Blessed are you when people insult you, persecute you and falsely say all kinds of evil against you because of me.

Rejoice and be glad, because great is your reward in heaven, for in the same way they persecuted the prophets who were before you».

When Jesus climbed the mountain and sat down to announce the Beatitudes, there was a crowd in that environment, but only the disciples came to him to better hear his message. What do we, disciples of Jesus, hear today when we come to Jesus?

Blessed are the «*poor in spirit*» who know how to live with little, but always trusting in God. Blessed is a church poor in spirit; it will have fewer problems because it will be more attentive to the needy and live the gospel more freely. The kingdom of heaven is hers.

Happy are «*the meek*» who empty their hearts of resentment and aggression. Blessed is a church full of meekness. It will be a gift to this world full of violence. She will inherit the promised land.

Blessed are those who «*weep*» for their sins and sufferings. With them we can create a better and more dignified world. Blessed is a church that mourns for her errors, because she will be on the road to conversion. One day she will be consoled by God.

Blessed are those who «*hunger and thirst for justice*», those who have not lost the desire to be more just nor the desire to make the world more decent. Blessed is the church that passionately seeks God's kingdom and His righteousness. She will nurture the best of the human spirit. One day her longing will be satisfied.

Happy are «*the merciful*» who act, work and live moved by compassion. They are those on earth, who most resemble the Father in heaven. Blessed is the church from which God has torn out the heart of stone and given it a heart of flesh. She will receive mercy.

Blessed are those who «*work for peace*» with patience and faith, seeking the good of all. Blessed is the church that brings into the world peace, not discord, reconciliation and not confrontation. She will be a «daughter of God».

Blessed are those who, «*persecuted for justice*», respond with meekness to injustices and offenses. They help us to overcome evil with good. Blessed is the church when persecuted because she follows Jesus. Hers is the kingdom of heaven.

4

The Courage of Not Being Perfect — If the Salt Becomes Tasteless…

MATTHEW 5:13-16

FIFTH SUNDAY OF ORDINARY TIME

«*"You are the salt of the earth. But if the salt loses its saltiness, how can it be made salty again? It is not good for anything, except to be thrown out and trampled by men.*

"You are the light of the world. A city on a hill cannot be hidden. Neither do people light a lamp and put it under a bowl. Instead they put it on its stand, and it gives light to everyone in the house. In the same way, let your light shine before men, that they may see your good deeds and praise your Father in heaven"».

It is a human tendency to want to appear more intelligent, kinder and more respectable than we really are. We live our lives trying to hide our failings in order to pretend before others and ourselves to have a perfection we do not possess.

Psychologists say that this tendency is a defense mechanism to maintain our self-respect when faced with the possible superiority of others. What we lack is the real self-affirmation that comes from a life of dignity. Instead, we fill our lives with a lot of talk and all kinds of explanations. We are incapable of giving our children an example of an honorable life, and we fill our days indoctrinating them, demanding from them what we do not practice.

We are not consistent with our Christian faith, and we try to justify ourselves by criticizing those who have abandoned religious practice. We are not witnesses of the gospel, but we are given to preaching it to others. Perhaps we need to begin by patiently recognizing our shortcomings and inconsistencies in order to appear before the world with only the truth of our lives. If we have the courage to accept our mediocrity, we will be open to the action of that God who can still transform our lives.

Jesus speaks of the danger that salt will become tasteless. St. John of the Cross puts it differently: «God forbid that the salt should begin to disappear, which, although it would seem from the outside that it works, would in fact be of no use, for it is certain that good works cannot be done except through the power of God».

In order to be the *salt of the earth*, what is important is not activity, busyness, or superficial leadership, but good works born of the love of that God who works in us.

We ought in the heart of the church to listen with deep attention to these words of the same John of the Cross: «Know, then, those of you who are very active and think of covering the world with their preaching and good works, that they would do the church much more good and would please God more… if they would spend half that time in being with God in prayer».

Otherwise, according to the same mystical doctor, it is to work hard and achieve little or nothing and, worse still, cause harm. In the midst of so much activity and exertion where are our «good works»?

5

Thou Shalt Not Kill

∽

MATTHEW 5:17-37

SIXTH SUNDAY OF ORDINARY TIME

«"*Do not think that I have come to abolish the Law or the Prophets; I have not come to abolish them but to fulfill them. I tell you the truth, until heaven and earth disappear, not the smallest letter, not the least stroke of a pen, will by any means disappear from the Law until everything is accomplished. Anyone who breaks one of the least of these commandments and teaches others to do the same will be called least in the kingdom of heaven, but whoever practices and teaches these commands will be called great in the kingdom of heaven. For I tell you that unless your righteousness surpasses that of the Pharisees and teachers of the law, you will certainly not enter the kingdom of heaven.*

"You have heard that it was said to the people long ago, 'Do not murder, and anyone who murders will be subject to judgment'. But I tell you that anyone who is angry with his brother will be subject to judgment. And anyone who says to his brother, 'Raca', is answerable to the Sanhedrin. But anyone who says, 'You fool!' will be in danger of the fire of hell.

"Therefore, if you are offering your gift at the altar and there remember that your brother has something against you, leave there your gift there in front of the altar. First go and be reconciled to your brother; then come and offer your gift.

"Settle matters quickly with your adversary who is taking you to court. Do it with him while you are still with him on the way, or he may hand you over to the judge, and the judge may

hand you over to the officer, and you may be thrown into prison. I tell you the truth, you will not get out until you have paid the last penny.

"You have heard what it was said, 'Do not commit adultery'. But I tell you that anyone who looks at a woman lustfully has already committed adultery with her in his heart. If your right eye causes you to sin, gouge it out and throw it away. It is better to lose one part of your body than for your whole body to be thrown into hell. And if your right hand causes you to sin, cut it off and throw it away. It is better to lose one part of your body than for your whole body to go to hell.

"It has been said, 'Anyone who divorces his wife must give her a certificate of divorce'. But I tell you that anyone who divorces his wife, except for marital unfaithfulness, causes her to become an adulteress, and anyone who marries the divorced woman commits adultery.

"Again, you have heard that it was said to the people long ago, 'Do not break your oath, but keep your oaths you have made to the Lord'. But I tell you, Do not swear at all: either by heaven, for it is God's throne; or by the earth, for it is his footstool; or by Jerusalem, for it is the city of the Great King. And do not swear by your head, for you cannot make one hair either white or black. Simply let your 'Yes' be 'Yes', and your 'No', 'No'; anything beyond this comes from the evil one"».

It is indeed terrifying to read the annual reports of Amnesty International, published every year with its usual thoroughness, on the violation of human rights in the world. Tens of thousands of people die annually: victims of mass killings, secret executions, summary trials, or as a result of inhuman torture. Some were killed at the doors of their houses, in mosques, or in churches. Others were eliminated in police stations, secret cells, military barracks or government premises. Many of these people were executed solely for their political or religious convictions or because of their color, ethnic origin or language.

It is especially heart-rending to learn of the attempts to cover up so much abuse: night executions, enforced disappearances, destruction of evidence, intervention of death squads, secret paramilitary forces, suppression of impartial investigations. According to the data, the 1980's were characterized by an extraordinary number of mass and individual killings committed precisely by government forces. However, the biblical imperative «Thou shalt not kill», so radically embraced and preached by Jesus, continues to this day to be systematically violated in the world, even by those who have the duty to protect the lives of people.

What can each of us do when faced with such worldwide brutality? How can we help raise international awareness and react more forcefully against such deplorable crimes? A simple but effective response is to collaborate with the activities that Amnesty International carries on so tirelessly. The work of this prestigious, independent organization is focused on the following tasks:

• To free «prisoners of conscience» who were not involved in violence or did not advocate it, by bringing pressure on the authorities through letters and articles, and alerting the public to the existence of forgotten prisoners.

• To campaign for impartial trials for all political prisoners and to protect them against injustice and arbitrary action.

• To investigate and denounce torture and inhuman and degrading treatment of any category of prisoners.

• To fight for the abolition of the death penalty still in force in more than a hundred countries and to conduct campaigns to stay the imminent execution of any prisoner.

6

Cordiality — If You Greet Only Your Brothers...

MATTHEW 5:38-48

SEVENTH SUNDAY OF ORDINARY TIME

«*"You have heard that it was said, 'Eye for eye, and tooth for tooth'. But I tell you, Do not resist an evil person. If someone strikes you on the right cheek, turn to him the other also. And if someone wants to sue you and take your tunic, let him have your cloak as well. If someone forces you to go one mile, go with him two miles. Give to the one who asks you, and do not turn away from the one who wants to borrow from you.*

"You have heard that it was said, 'Love your neighbor and hate your enemy'. But I tell you: Love your enemies and pray for those who persecute you, that you may be sons of your Father in heaven. He causes his sun to rise on the evil and the good, and sends his rain on the righteous and the unrighteous. If you love those who love you, what reward will you get? Are not even the tax collectors doing that? And if you greet only your brothers, what are you doing more than others? Do not even pagans do that? Be perfect, therefore, as your heavenly Father is perfect"».

The best measure of Christian love is not the external, sensible manifestation of feelings, but the care that is shown for the good of another. In general, humble service of a needy person involves love more than a lot of effusive words. Unfortunately, we have placed so much stress on the effort of the will that we have come to strip charity of its affective content. Nevertheless, Christian love that is born in the depths of a person also inspires and directs the feelings and is manifested in heartfelt affection.

To love our neighbor demands we do good to that person, but it also implies accepting, respecting, discovering what is lovable in that person, and letting him/her experience our acceptance and love. Christian charity inspires a person to adopt an attitude of warm sympathy, care and affection, while overcoming feelings of hostility, indifference and rejection.

Naturally, our personal manner of being loving is conditioned by the sensitivity, affective richness and ability of each of us to communicate with others. But Christian love promotes cordiality, sincere affection and friendship between people. This cordiality is not merely external courtesy required by a proper social upbringing, nor is it the spontaneous affinity we have for people we take a liking to, but it is the sincere attitude of one who has been purified and inspired by Christian love.

Perhaps we do not stress enough the importance that the fostering of this cordiality has within the family circle, in the work place, and in all our relationships. Cordiality helps people to feel good about themselves, eases tensions and conflicts, furthers understanding, strengthens friendships, and helps fraternity grow. Cordiality helps people rid themselves of feelings of selfishness and rejection, because it is directly opposed to our tendency to dominate, manipulate or make others suffer. Those who know how to accept and communicate affection in a healthy and generous way create around them a more human world in which to live.

Jesus insists on having this cordiality shown not only to a friend or to a person we like, but even to someone who rejects us. Remember his words, which show us the way he thought and behaved: «If you greet only your brothers, are you doing anything exceptional?»

7

The Golden Calf — You Cannot Serve God and Money

MATTHEW 6:24-34

EIGHTH SUNDAY OF ORDINARY TIME

«*"No one can serve two masters. Either he will hate the one and love the other, or he will be devoted to one and despise the other. You cannot serve both God and Money.*

Therefore I tell you, do not worry about your life, what you will eat or drink; or about your body, what you will wear. Is not life more important than food, and the body more important than clothes? Look at the birds of the air; they do not sow or reap or store away in barns, and yet your heavenly Father feeds them. Are you not more valuable than they? Who of you by worrying can add a single hour to his life?

And why do you worry about clothes? See how the lilies of the field grow. They do not labor or spin. Yet I tell you that not even Solomon in all his splendor was dressed like one of these. If that is how God clothes the grass of the field, which is here today and tomorrow is thrown into the fire will not he much more clothe you, O you of little faith? So do not worry, saying, 'What shall we eat?' or 'What shall we drink?' or 'What shall we wear?' For the pagans run after all these things, and your heavenly Father knows that you need them. But seek first his kingdom and his righteousness, and all these things will be given to you as well. Therefore do not worry about tomorrow, for tomorrow will worry about itself, Each day has enough trouble of its own"».

The fall of the communist regimes in the East has shown that you cannot establish justice by destroying freedom. Justice and freedom are inseparable. Only in free countries is there the possibility of bringing about a more just world.

But those so-called free countries of the West are more enslaved than ever to a «heartless capitalism», which, in order to secure relative prosperity for a billion people, has not hesitated to condemn to misery the other four and a half billion who inhabit the earth. The facts show that gradually but inexorably «the cake is shared by increasingly fewer mouths».

The Europe that some years ago extended generous hospitality to foreign workers, who came to do work that no one else wanted to do, is now passing laws that create insurmountable barriers against the hunger that we ourselves have helped to create in the Third World.

Who in Europe cares that two entire continents, Africa and Latin America, today have a standard of living lower than ten years ago? Who is going to be concerned for the fourteen million children who die of hunger every year, while in this Europe racist movements keep increasing, sometimes shamelessly, and almost always disguised in a thousand different forms?

We became accustomed to watching from the comfort of our couches as those sick, hungry, desperate Albanians arriving at Italian ports were expelled. Nobody seemed to react very convincingly when they saw the spectacle of those Africans who attempted the impossible by trying to cross over, only to end up at the bottom of the sea or in the prisons of the coast guards of Tarifa.

The church today cannot proclaim the gospel in Europe without unmasking all this inhumanity and without asking the questions that almost nobody wants to ask themselves:

• Why do people die of hunger, if God has placed in our hands resources of the earth enough to feed everyone?

• Why must we be competitive rather than human?

• Why must competition define relations between people and between nations rather than solidarity?

• Why must we accept as something logical and inevitable an economic system which, in order to obtain prosperity for a few, marginalizes and plunges into poverty so many victims as if it were an intrinsic necessity?

• Why must we foster consumerism as a «philosophy of life,» if it triggers an insatiable spiral of artificial needs, which in turn is draining us of our human spirit and sensibilities?

• Why must we continue to foster the worship of money as though it were the only god that offers security, power and happiness?

• Is this perhaps the «new religion» that will make modern man advance to new heights of greater humanity?

These are not questions for others. Each of us must listen in our consciences to the echo of those words of Jesus: «*You cannot serve God and Money*».

8

How Are We Building?

MATTHEW 7: 21-27

NINTH SUNDAY OF ORDINARY TIME

«*"Not everyone who says to me, 'Lord, Lord', will enter the kingdom of heaven, but only he who does the will of my Father who is in heaven. Many will say to me on that day, 'Lord, Lord, did we not prophesy in your name, and in your name drive out demons and perform many miracles?' Then I will tell them plainly, 'I never knew you. Away from me, you evildoers!' Therefore everyone who hears these words of mine and puts them into practice is like a wise man who built his house on the rock. The rain came down, the streams rose, and the winds blew and beat against that house; yet it did not fall, because it had its foundation on the rock. But everyone who hears these words of mine and does not put them into practice is like a foolish man who built his house on sand. The rain came down, the streams rose, and the winds blew and beat against that house, and it fell with a great crash"*».

The followers of Jesus gave the words of Jesus a transcendental importance. Heaven and earth will pass away but never the words of Jesus They had seen the power of that word in Galilee which freed people from sickness, suffering, sin and fears. Now in Christian communities they saw it bring truth into their lives, resurrected them from within, and filled them with life and peace.

So Matthew takes a parable in which he emphasizes something that today we Christians must remember continually, very clearly and concretely: to be Christian is to put into practice the words of Jesus and to make his gospel a reality. If we do not do this, our Christianity will be «foolish». It will have no meaning.

The parable is short, symmetrical and rhythmical. It has probably been composed to facilitate catechetical teaching. It is important that everyone knows that the first thing to be done in the Christian community is to listen to and to put into practice the words that come from Jesus. There is no better way to build a church of followers or a better world.

A wise man does not build a house just any way. He is concerned with what's most important: to build on firm rock. The foolish man, on the other hand, does not think about what he is doing; he builds on sand at the bottom of the valley. When the winter rains come, bringing swollen rivers and stormy winds, the house built on rock stands firm, while the one built on sand is totally washed away.

The parable is a serious warning and obliges us Christians to ask ourselves whether we are building the church of Jesus on rock, by listening to his words and putting them into practice, or whether we are building on unsafe sand that has neither the firmness nor the guarantee of the gospel.

The current crisis is exposing the truth or the lies of our Christian lives. Neither sociological analysis nor instinctive reactions will do. Has not the time arrived to make an examination of conscience at all levels in our communities and in the church, to call into question false complacency and pinpoint how we have fallen short of practicing the gospel? It is not enough to say to Jesus, «Lord, Lord», if we do not do the will of the Father.

9

Above All, Mercy

MATTHEW 9: 9-13

TENTH SUNDAY OF ORDINARY TIME

«As Jesus went on from there, he saw a man named Matthew sitting at the tax collector's booth. "Follow me", he told him, and Matthew got up and followed him.

While Jesus was having dinner at Matthew's house, many tax collectors and "sinners" came and ate with him and his disciples. When the Pharisees saw this, they asked his disciples, "Why does your teacher eat with tax collectors and 'sinners'?" On hearing this, Jesus said, "It is not the healthy who need a doctor, but the sick. But go and learn what this means: 'I desire mercy, not sacrifice'. For I have not come to call the righteous, but sinners"».

It is an unusual scene. For the most religious group in Israel, this is an unforgivable scandal. Jesus is seated at table in the house of Matthew together with his disciples. But they are not alone. Many publicans and sinners join in the banquet and sit with him. Jesus is lost in the company of a whole lot of sinners. The account notes that there were «many». They are all seated at the same table, mingled with the disciples.

The most religious group reacts immediately. Why does Jesus behave so scandalously? Sinners are undesirable and contemptible people. They are the cause of all the evils that the chosen people suffer. It is best to exclude those who do not live according to the Covenant —the group of sinners and prostitutes, for example. How can a man of God live on such friendly terms with them?

Jesus pays no attention to their criticism. All are invited to his table, because God is the God of all, even of those ostracized by religion. These meals represent the grand project of a God who offers his salvation to all. Religious officials cannot fathom or explain the mercy of the Father.

Jesus responds to the allegations through the depths of his own attitude. The manner in which he regards those who, for different reasons, do not come up to the moral standards of those who live in accordance with the prescriptions of the Law, is important. He sees them as «sick», more as «victims» than as guilty, more in need of help than of condemnation. That is how Jesus regards them.

Equally important is the way he accepts them. It is not the healthy who need a doctor, but the sick. The first thing they need is not a teacher of the Law to judge them, but a friendly doctor who will help them to get cured. Jesus saw himself not as a judge passing sentence, but as a doctor who comes to seek and save those who are lost.

This behavior is not the sympathetic attitude of a good prophet. Here he reveals the way God treats us. That is why Jesus says to us, «Drop your accusations and learn from me the meaning of the words of the prophet Hosea: God wants mercy and not sacrifice and your cult».

If we do not learn from Jesus that the important thing for God is always mercy, we will lack something essential for a disciple of his. A church without mercy does not follow in the footsteps of Jesus.

10

Authority to Do Good

«When he saw the crowds, he had compassion on them, because they were harassed and helpless, like sheep without a shepherd. Then he said to his disciples, "The harvest is plentiful but the workers are few. Ask the Lord of the harvest, therefore, to send out workers into his harvest field".

He called his twelve disciples to him and gave them authority to drive out evil spirits and to heal every disease and sickness. These twelve Jesus sent out with the following instructions: "Do not go among the Gentiles or enter any town of the Samaritans. Go rather to the lost sheep of Israel. As you go, preach this message: 'The kingdom of heaven is near'. Heal the sick, raise the dead, cleanse those who have leprosy, drive out demons. Freely you have received, freely give"».

Jesus paid close attention to the people in need whom he met on his travels. He notices the paralyzed man in Capernaum, the two blind men of Jericho, or the old woman bent by a disease, and *«his heart is filled with pity»*. He cannot pass them by without doing something to relieve their suffering.

Moreover, the Gospels present him frequently with his gaze fixed on the crowds. He saw the people hungry, beset with all kinds of diseases and sicknesses, and the same thing always happened: he felt compassion for them. But there was something else that hurt him in a special way. Matthew reminds us: *«On seeing the multitudes he had pity on them for they were weak and abandoned like sheep without a shepherd»*. Neither the representatives of Rome nor the religious leaders of Jerusalem cared for those people of the villages.

This compassion of Jesus is not a passing sentiment. It is the way he saw the people and sought to do good. It is his way of incarnating God's mercy. His decision to call the twelve apostles and send them to the lost sheep of Israel was born of this compassion.

For that purpose he himself gives them authority; but what he gives them is not a sacred power for them to use arbitrarily as they wished. It is not a power to govern people and nations like the Romans did. It is a power whose purpose is to do good, driving out evil spirits and healing every kind of disease and sickness.

All the authority that is in the church derives from and is founded on the compassion of Jesus for the people. Its purpose is to heal, to alleviate suffering, and to do good. It is a gift from Jesus. Those who exercise it must do it «for free» because the church is a gift of Jesus to the nations.

So the disciples must preach what he preached and nothing else. «*Preach this message: the kingdom of heaven is near*», so that the people can hear this news and take part in God's project. They must do so by bringing health, life, community, and by freeing the possessed. This is what the four commands of Jesus suggest: «*Heal the sick, raise the dead, cleanse those who have leprosy, drive out demons*».

11
Without Fear

MATTHEW 10: 26-33

TWELFTH SUNDAY OF ORDINARY TIME

« "*So do not be afraid of them. There is nothing concealed that will not be disclosed, or hidden that will not be made known. What I tell you in the dark, speak in the daylight; what is whispered in your ear, proclaim from the roofs. Do not be afraid of those who kill the body but cannot kill the soul. Rather, be afraid*

*of the One who can destroy both soul and body in hell. Are not
two sparrows sold for a penny? Yet not one of them will fall to
the ground apart from the will of your Father. And even the
very hairs of your head are all numbered. So don't be afraid;
you are worth more than many sparrows. Whoever acknowledges me before men, I will also acknowledge him before my
Father in heaven. But whoever disowns me before men, I will
disown him before my Father in heaven"».*

The memory of the execution of Jesus was still fresh in the
Christian communities. Various accounts of his passion were
in circulation. Everyone knew that it was dangerous to follow someone who had ended his life so infamously. They remembered a saying of Jesus: «*The disciple is not greater than
his master*». If they have called him Beelzebub what will they
not say of his followers?

Jesus did not want his disciples to have any illusions about
their future with him. Nobody could think of truly following him without in some way sharing his fate. At some time
someone will reject, ill-treat, insult or condemn them. What
should they do?

His answer flows from within him: «*Do not be afraid*».
Fear is bad. It should never paralyze his disciples. They must
never keep silent. They must not on any account stop propa-
gating his message.

Jesus is going to explain to them how they have to face
persecution. With him the revelation of the Good News of
God has begun. They must trust God. What is now covered
and hidden from many will one day be plainly known. The
mystery of God will be made known as his love of humankind
and his project for a happier life for all.

The followers of Christ are called to take an active part
from now on in that process of revelation: «*What I tell you in
the dark, speak in the daylight; what is whispered in your ear,
proclaim from the roofs*». What he explains to them at sunset
before retiring for the night must be broadcast without fear

in the light of day. What I say to you in your ears, proclaim it from the roofs. What is whispered in your ears so that it reaches your hearts, you must make public.

Jesus insists that they should not be afraid. The person who is with me has nothing to fear. The last judgment will be a pleasant surprise for him. The Father in heaven will be the judge, the one who loves you without limits. I myself will be your advocate who will be on your side. Can anyone inspire in us more confidence in times of trial?

Jesus thought of his followers as a group of believers who would side with him without fear. Why don't we feel entirely free to open up new pathways more faithful to Jesus? Why do we not dare to set forth in simple, clear, and concrete terms the essential demands of the gospel?

12
Ready to Suffer

MATTHEW 10: 37-42

THIRTEENTH SUNDAY OF ORDINARY TIME

« *"Anyone who loves his father or mother more than me is not worthy of me; anyone who loves his son or daughter more than me is not worthy of me; and anyone who does not take his cross and follow me is not worthy of me. Whoever finds his life will lose it, and whoever loses his life for my sake will find it. He who receives you receives me, and he who receives me receives the one who sent me.*

"Anyone who receives a prophet because he is a prophet will receive a prophet's reward, and anyone who receives a righteous man because he is a righteous man will receive a righteous man's reward. And if anyone gives even a cup of cold water to one of these little ones because he is my disciple, I tell you the truth, he will certainly not lose his reward" ».

Jesus did not want to see anyone suffer. Suffering is bad. Jesus never sought it, either for himself or for anyone else. On the contrary, all his life he fought against the suffering and evil that has harmed people so much.

The Gospels show him always fighting the suffering that lies behind sickness, injustice, loneliness, despair or sinfulness. Jesus lived as a man committed to eliminating suffering, ending injustice and infusing strength in people so they could live.

But seeking the good and happiness of all brings with it many problems. Jesus knew this from experience. It is not possible to be with those who suffer and to seek the good of the most vulnerable without provoking the reaction of those who have no interest in any change. It is impossible to be with the crucified without one day being crucified oneself.

Jesus never hid this from his followers. On various occasions he used a disquieting metaphor that the evangelist Matthew summed up thus: «*Anyone who does not take up his cross and follow me is not worthy of me*». He could not have chosen more shocking language. Everyone had seen the terrible reality of a man condemned to death, naked and helpless, carrying on his shoulders the horizontal beam of the cross to the place of execution where the vertical beam planted in the earth awaited it.

To carry the cross was part of the ritual of crucifixion. Its aim was to have the condemned man appear guilty before the public, as a man unworthy of continuing to live with his people. Everyone could rest secure seeing him dead.

The disciples were trying to understand him. What Jesus was telling them amounted more or less to this: «If you follow me, you must be ready to be rejected. What will happen to me will happen to you. In the eyes of many you will be held guilty. They will condemn you. They will want you not to disturb them. You will have to carry your cross. Then you will be more like me. You will be worthy followers of me. You will share the fate of the crucified. With them you will one day enter the kingdom of God». To carry the cross is not to seek «crosses» but to accept crucifixion that will befall us if we follow in the footsteps of Jesus. Nothing could be clearer.

13
Three Offers from Jesus

MATTHEW 11: 25-30

FOURTEENTH SUNDAY OF ORDINARY TIME

«At that time Jesus said, "I praise you, Father, Lord of heaven and earth, because you have hidden these things from the wise and learned, and revealed them to little children. Yes, Father, for this was your good pleasure. All things have been committed to me by my Father. No one knows the Son except the Father, and no one knows the Father except the Son and those to whom the Son chooses to reveal him. Come to me, all you who are weary and burdened, and I will give you rest. Take my yoke upon you and learn from me, for I am gentle and humble in heart, and you will find rest for your souls. For my yoke is easy and my burden is light"».

One day Jesus surprised everyone by thanking God for his success with the simple folk and for his failure with the teachers of the Law, the scribes and the priests. *«I praise you, Father, Lord of heaven and earth, because you have hidden these things from the wise and learned, and revealed them to little children».* Jesus seems happy with the situation. *«Yes, Father, for this was your good pleasure».*

That is God's way of revealing his inner thoughts. Simple and ignorant folk, those who have no access to great learning, those who are not considered important in the religion of the temple, are opening themselves to God with pure hearts. They are willing to be taught by Jesus. The Father is revealing his love through him. They understand Jesus as they do no one else.

However, the learned and the clever ones don't understand anything at all. They have their own learned opinion of God and of religion. They think they know everything. They do not learn anything new from Jesus. Their closed minds and hardened hearts prevent them from being open to the Father through his Son.

Jesus finishes his prayer but continues thinking of the simple folk. They are oppressed by the powerful leaders of Sepphoris and Tiberias and find no solace in the religion of the temple. Their life is hard, and the doctrine they are taught by the learned makes it even more difficult. Jesus makes them three offers.

The first offer: «*Come to me all you who are weary and burdened*». It is directed to all who experience religion as a burden, those who are burdened by doctrines that prevent them from experiencing the joy of salvation. If they come into vital contact with Jesus they will find immediate solace: «I will give you rest».

The second offer: «*Take my yoke upon you… for my yoke is bearable and my burden light*». Change your burden. Cast off that of the wise and prudent because it is not bearable, and take on the yoke of Jesus, which makes life more bearable. Not because Jesus exacts less. He exacts more, but in a different way. He exacts what is essential: the love that frees us from that which does us harm.

The third offer: «*Learn from me because I am meek and humble of heart*». Learn to fulfill the demands of the Law and religion by understanding them in the spirit of Jesus. Jesus does not complicate life. He makes it more simple and humble. He does not oppress, but frees us to live it in a more dignified and human manner. To meet Jesus is to find rest.

14

Hearing, They Do Not Hear

MATTHEW 13: 1-23

FIFTEENTH SUNDAY OF ORDINARY TIME

«*That same day Jesus went out of the house and sat by the lake. Such large crowds gathered around him that he got into a boat and sat in it, while all the people stood on the shore. Then he told them many things in parables, saying: "A farmer went out to sow his seed. As he was scattering the seed, some fell along the path, and the birds came and ate it up. Some fell on rocky places, where it did not have much soil. It sprang up quickly, because the soil was shallow. But when the sun came up, the plants were scorched, and they withered because they had no root. Other seed fell among thorns, which grew up and choked the plants. Still other seed fell on good soil, where it produced a crop —a hundred, sixty or thirty times what was sown. He who has ears, let him hear".*

The disciples came to him and asked, "Why do you speak to the people in parables?" He replied, "The knowledge of the secrets of the kingdom of heaven has been given to you, but not to them. Whoever has will be given more, and he will have an abundance. Whoever does not have, even what he has will be taken from him. This is why I speak to them in parables: Though seeing, they do not see; though hearing, they do not hear or understand. In them is fulfilled the prophecy of Isaiah: 'You will be ever hearing but never understanding; you will be ever seeing but never perceiving. For this people's heart has become calloused; they hardly hear with their ears, and they have closed their eyes. Otherwise they might see with their eyes, hear with their ears, understand with their hearts and turn, and I would heal them'. But blessed are your eyes because they see, and your ears because they hear. For I tell you the truth, many prophets and righteous men longed to see what you see but did not see it, and to hear what you hear but did not hear it. Listen then to what the parable of the sower means: When anyone hears the message about the kingdom and does not understand it, the evil one comes and snatches away what was sown in his heart. This is the seed sown along the path. The one who received the seed that fell on rocky places is the man who hears the word and at once receives it with joy. But since he has no root, he lasts only a short time. When trouble or persecution comes because of the word, he quickly falls away. The one who received the seed that fell among the thorns is the man who hears the word, but the worries of this life and the deceitfulness of wealth choke it, making it unfruitful. But the one who received the seed that fell on good soil is the man who hears the word and understands it. He produces a crop, yielding a hundred, sixty or thirty times what was sown».

The parables of Jesus have always delighted his followers. The Gospels have preserved about 40 of them. Most probably these are the ones Jesus repeated more often or those that remained imprinted more strongly in the hearts and memories of his disciples. How should we understand these parables? How do we get their message?

First of all, Matthew reminds us that the parables were «sown» in the world by Jesus. He left his home to teach his message to the people, and his first parable begins precisely like this: «*A sower went out to sow*». The sower is Jesus. His parables are a call to understand and live life just the way he understood and lived it. If we do not identify with Jesus we will hardly understand his parables.

What Jesus sows is the message of the kingdom. Matthew says so. Every parable is an invitation to pass from an old conventional world that is hardly human, to a new land full of life, just as God wants it for his children. Jesus called it the kingdom of God. If we do not work for a more human world, how will we understand his parables?

Jesus sows his message in the heart, that is, in the inner depths of the person. That's where true conversion takes place. It is not enough to preach the parables. If the hearts of Christians and the church are not open to Jesus, we will never experience his power to transform us.

Jesus does not discriminate against anyone. What happens is that to those who are disciples and walk in his footsteps, God grants them an understanding of the secrets of the kingdom, but not to those who don't. The disciples have the key to understanding the parables. Their knowledge of God's plan will only get deeper. But those who fail to take the step of following Jesus and continue without making an option for Jesus will not understand his message, and the little they do hear, they stand to lose.

When we end up living with a closed heart, we have a problem. For what happens then is inevitable. We will have ears, but we will not hear. We will have eyes, but we will not see Jesus. Our hearts will not understand anything. How do we sow the gospel in our Christian communities? What will inspire us all to welcome the sower?

15

Like Leaven

MATTHEW 13: 24-43

SIXTEENTH SUNDAY OF ORDINARY TIME

«*Jesus told them another parable: "The kingdom of heaven is like a man who sowed good seed in his field. But while everyone was sleeping, his enemy came and sowed weeds among the wheat, and went away. When the wheat sprouted and formed heads, then the weeds also appeared. The owner's servants came to him and said, 'Sir, didn't you sow good seed in your field? Where then did the weeds come from?' 'An enemy did this', he replied. The servants asked him, 'Do you want us to go* and pull them up?' 'No', he answered, 'because while you are pulling the weeds, you may root up the wheat with them. Let both grow together until the harvest. At that time I will tell the harvesters: First collect the weeds and tie them in bundles to be burned; then gather the wheat and bring it into my barn'".

He told them another parable: "The kingdom of heaven is like a mustard seed, which a man took and planted in his field. Though it is the smallest of all your seeds, yet when it grows, it is the largest of garden plants and becomes a tree, so that the birds of the air come and perch in its branches".

He told them still another parable: "The kingdom of heaven is like yeast that a woman took and mixed into a large amount of flour until it worked all through the dough".

Jesus spoke all these things to the crowd in parables; he did not say anything to them without using a parable. So was fulfilled what was spoken through the prophet: "I will open my mouth in parables, I will utter things hidden since the creation of the world".

Then he left the crowd and went into the house. His disciples came to him and said, "Explain to us the parable of the weeds in the field". He answered, "The one who sowed the good seed is the Son of Man. The field is the world, and the good seed stands for the sons of the kingdom. The weeds are the sons of the evil one, and the enemy who sows them is the devil. The harvest is the end of the age, and the harvesters are angels. As the weeds are pulled up and burned in the fire, so it will be at the end of the age. The Son of Man will send out his angels, and they will weed out of his kingdom everything that causes sin and all who do evil. They will throw them into the fiery furnace, where there will be weeping and gnashing of teeth. Then the righteous will shine like the sun in the kingdom of their Father. He who has ears, let him hear"».

Jesus repeated it over and over again: God is here trying to change the world. His kingdom is coming. It was not easy to believe Jesus. The people were waiting for something more spectacular. Where are the «signs from heaven» of which the apocalyptic writers speak? Where can you see the power of God come down on the wicked?

Jesus had to teach them to perceive his presence in a different form. He still remembered the scene that he had seen in the patio of his house. His mother and the other women would arise early on the eve of the Sabbath to prepare bread for the whole week. It suggested to Jesus the motherly work of God in placing his leaven in the world.

The kingdom of God comes about like the leaven that a woman «hides» in the dough so that the whole mass gets fermented. That's how God acts. He does not come from the outside to impose his power like the emperor of Rome, but to transform human life from within in a silent and hidden manner.

This is the way God is: he does not impose, but transforms; does not dominate, but attracts. Thus, those who work with him in his project must act like leaven by bringing in his truth, his justice and his love in a humble way, but with transforming power.

As followers of Jesus we cannot present ourselves in this society as outsiders trying to impose ourselves and dominate and control those who do not think like us. That is not the way to open the way to the kingdom of God. We must become part of the society, sharing the uncertainties, crises and contradictions of today's world, and contributing to it our lives transformed by the gospel.

We must learn to live our lives as a minority of faithful witnesses to Jesus. What the church needs is not more social or political power, but more humility to allow ourselves to be transformed by Jesus in order to be the ferment of a more human world.

16

Decision

MATTHEW 13: 44-52

SEVENTEENTH SUNDAY OF ORDINARY TIME

« *"The kingdom of heaven is like treasure hidden in a field. When a man found it, he hid it again, and then in his joy went and sold all he had and bought that field. Again, the kingdom of heaven is like a merchant looking for fine pearls. When he found one of great value, he went away and sold everything he had and bought it.*

"Once again, the kingdom of heaven is like a net that was let down into the lake and caught all kinds of fish. When it was full, the fishermen pulled it up on the shore. Then they sat down and collected the good fish in baskets, but threw the bad away. This is how it will be at the end of the age. The angels will come and separate the wicked from the righteous and throw them into the fiery furnace, where there will be weeping and gnashing of teeth.

"Have you understood all these things?" Jesus asked. "Yes", they replied. He said to them, "Therefore every teacher of the law who has been instructed about the kingdom of heaven is like the owner of a house who brings out of his storeroom new treasures as well as old"».

115

It wasn't easy to believe in Jesus. Some people were attracted by his message. Others, on the other hand, had a lot of doubts. Was it reasonable to follow Jesus, or was it madness? Today it is the same. Is it worth committing oneself to the project of humanizing the world, or is it more practical to look for one's own well-being? In the meantime life can pass us by without our making any decision.

Jesus tells two parables to gain the hearts of those peasants. A poor worker is digging in a field he doesn't own. Suddenly he finds a hidden treasure. It is not difficult to imagine his surprise and joy. He doesn't think twice. Full of joy he sells all he has and goes off with the treasure.

The same thing happens to a wealthy merchant dealing in precious pearls. Suddenly he finds one of incalculable value. His instinct as an expert does not fail him. He makes a quick decision. He sells all he has and goes off with the pearl.

The kingdom of God is hidden. Many have not yet discovered the grand project God has for a new world. However it is not an inaccessible mystery. It is hidden in Jesus, in his life and in his message. A Christian community that has not discovered the kingdom of God does not know the purpose of its own origin in Jesus.

The discovery of the kingdom of God changes the life of the one who discovers it. His joy is unmistakable. He has discovered the essence of life, the best Jesus offers, the value that can change his life. If Christians do not discover the project of Jesus, there will be no joy in the church.

The two main characters in the parables make the same decision: they sell all they have. There is nothing more important than to seek the kingdom of God and his righteousness. Everything else is secondary and relative and must be subordinated to the project of God. The most important decision that we must make in the church and in Christian communities is to rid ourselves of so much that is accidental in order to commit ourselves to the kingdom of God, to strip ourselves of what is superfluous, to forget other pursuits, to learn to lose in order to gain in authenticity. If we do this we will be working together for the conversion of the church.

17
You Give Them to Eat

MATTHEW 14:13-21

EIGHTEENTH SUNDAY OF ORDINARY TIME

«When Jesus heard what had happened, he withdrew by boat privately to a solitary place. Hearing of this, the crowds followed him on foot from the towns. When Jesus landed and saw a large crowd, he had compassion on them and healed their sick. As evening approached, the disciples came to him and said, "This is a remote place, and it's already getting late. Send the crowds away, so they can go to the villages and buy themselves some food". Jesus replied, "They do not need to go away. You give them something to eat". "We have here only five loaves of bread and two fish", they answered. "Bring them here to me", he said.

And he directed the people to sit down on the grass. Taking the five loaves and the two fish and looking up to heaven, he gave thanks and broke the loaves. Then he gave them to the disciples, and the disciples gave them to the people. They all ate and were satisfied, and the disciples picked up twelve basketfuls of broken pieces that were left over. The number of those who ate was about five thousand men, besides women and children».

The evangelist Matthew is not concerned with the details of the story. He is only interested in framing the scene by presenting Jesus in an attitude of compassion while in the midst of people. He does this on other occasions as well. This compassion is at the root of all his activity.

Jesus does not live with his back to the people, busy with religious duties and indifferent to the suffering of the people. *«He sees the crowds, he feels pity for them and he heals the sick».* His experience of God makes him act to relieve the suffering of those poor people and to satisfy their hunger. This is how the church that wants to make Jesus present in the world must live also.

Time is passing and Jesus is busy healing people. The disciples interrupt him to tell him: «*It's already getting late. Send the crowds away, so they can go to the villages and buy themselves some food*». They haven't learned anything from Jesus. They are unconcerned about the hungry, and they abandon them to economic laws controlled by landowners: «Let them buy themselves some food». What will they do, those who cannot buy?

Jesus replies with a terse order that self-satisfied Christians in rich countries do not even want to hear. «You give them something to eat». Instead of «buying», Jesus proposes «giving» something to eat. He couldn't have said it more forcefully. He goes about crying out to the Father: «Give us this day our daily bread». God wants all his children to have bread, even those who cannot buy it.

The disciples are unconvinced. Among the people there are just five loaves and two fishes. For Jesus that's enough. If we share what we have we can satisfy the hunger of all; there may even be twelve baskets left over. This is his alternative: a more human society that can share its bread with the hungry will have sufficient resources for all. In a world where millions of people die of hunger, Christians can only live in shame. The developed countries of the world do not have a Christian soul, for they send away as lawbreakers those who come looking for bread. Meanwhile in the church there are many who follow the way Jesus showed them; the majority, however, preoccupied with their affairs, debates, doctrines, and celebrations, are deaf to his call. Why call ourselves followers of Jesus?

18

Fear Has Entered the Church

MATTHEW 14: 22-33

NINETEENTH SUNDAY OF ORDINARY TIME

«Immediately Jesus made the disciples get into the boat and go on ahead of him to the other side, while he dismissed the crowd. After he had dismissed them, he went up on a mountainside by himself to pray. When evening came, he was there alone, but the boat was already a considerable distance from land, buffeted by the waves because the wind was against it. During the fourth watch of the night Jesus went out to them, walking on the lake. When the disciples saw him walking on the lake, they were terrified. "It's a ghost", they said, and cried out in fear. But Jesus immediately said to them: "Take courage! It is I. Don't be afraid". "Lord, if it's you", Peter replied, "tell me to come to you on the water". "Come", he said. Then Peter got down out of the boat, walked on the water and came toward Jesus. But when he saw the wind, he was afraid and, beginning to sink, cried out, "Lord, save me!" Immediately Jesus reached out his hand and caught him. "You of little faith", he said, "why did you doubt?" And when they climbed into the boat, the wind died down. Then those who were in the boat worshiped him, saying, "Truly you are the Son of God"».

Very probably Jesus used the difficulties they experienced journeying along the lake of Galilee to prepare his disciples to meet more severe trials in the future. Matthew works on one of those incidents to help Christian communities free themselves of «fears» and of their little «faith».

The disciples are by themselves. On this occasion Jesus is not with them. Their boat is very far from land, quite far from him, and a contrary wind keeps them from returning. Alone in the midst of a storm, what can they do without Jesus?

The boat is in a desperate situation. Matthew speaks of the darkness of the night, the force of the wind, and the danger of drowning in the sea. With this language of the Bible, which his readers knew quite well, he is describing the situation of those Christian communities threatened from outside by rejection and hostility, and tempted from within by fear and little faith. Isn't this our own situation today?

Between three and six at early dawn, Jesus comes to them walking on the water, but the disciples cannot recognize him. The fear in them makes them see a ghost. Fears are the greatest obstacle to know, love, and follow Jesus as the Son of God who is with us and saves us in times of crisis.

Jesus says the three words they need to hear: «*Take courage! It is I. Don't be afraid*». He wants to transmit to them his power, confidence and absolute faith in the Father. Peter is the first to react. His attitude is as always a model of trusting devotion and at the same time an example of fear and little faith. He walks securely on the water and then gets afraid; he goes confidently to Jesus, forgets his order to him, feels the force of the wind, and begins to sink.

Fear has entered the church and we do not know how to free ourselves of it. We are afraid of losing prestige and power and being rejected by society. We are afraid of one another. The hierarchy uses strong language, theologians lose their freedom, pastors prefer not to run risks, and the faithful are afraid of the future. At the root of these fears is our little faith in Jesus and our refusal to follow his footsteps. He himself helps us to look at ourselves: «*What little faith you have! Why did you doubt?*»

19

The Cry of the Woman

MATTHEW 15: 21-28

TWENTIETH SUNDAY OF ORDINARY TIME

«*Leaving that place, Jesus withdrew to the region of Tyre and Sidon. A Canaanite woman from that vicinity came to him, crying out, "Lord, Son of David, have mercy on me! My daughter is suffering terribly from demon-possession". Jesus did not answer a word. So his disciples came to him and urged him, "Send her away, for she keeps crying out after us". He answered, "I was sent only to the lost sheep of Israel". The woman came and knelt before him. "Lord, help me!" she said. He replied, "It is not right to take the children's bread and toss it to their dogs". "Yes, Lord", she said, "but even the dogs eat the crumbs that fall from their masters' table". Then Jesus answered, "Woman, you have great faith! Your request is granted". And her daughter was healed from that very hour*».

In the eighties when Matthew was writing his Gospel, the church had a serious problem: What should the followers of Jesus do? Should they continue to remain only within the confines of the Jewish culture and people or should they open out to the pagan world? Jesus had only worked within the borders of Israel. Summarily executed by the leaders of the temple, he was not able to do more. However, inquiring into his life, his disciples remembered two enlightening facts. Firstly, Jesus was able to discover a greater faith in the pagans than in his own followers. Secondly, Jesus had not restricted his compassion only to Jews. The God of compassion is the God of all.

It is a touching scene. A woman comes to meet Jesus. She does not belong to the chosen people. She is a pagan. She comes from the accursed Canaanites who had fought so often against Israel. She is nameless and alone. She doesn't have a husband or brothers to protect her. Perhaps she is an unmarried mother, or a widow, or has been abandoned by her people.

Matthew only highlights her faith. She is the first woman who speaks in his Gospel. Her whole life is summed up in a cry which expresses the depth of her misfortune. She follows the disciples, crying out. She doesn't stop crying out in spite of the silence of Jesus or the uneasiness of his disciples. The misfortune of her daughter, possessed by a rather nasty demon, has become her own pain. «*Lord, have mercy on me*».

At some point the woman meets up with the group, halts Jesus, prostrates herself, and on her knees says, «*Lord, help me*». She does not accept the explanations of Jesus about his purpose in Israel. She does not accept the ethnic, political, religious and gender exclusion of so many women suffering from being marginalized.

It is then that Jesus appears, in all his humility and greatness. «*Woman, you have great faith! Your request is granted*». The woman is right. All these other explanations are of no use. It is important to relieve suffering. Her request coincides with God's will.

What are we Christians doing when faced with the cries of so many women who are alone, marginalized, ill-treated, and forgotten? Do we push them aside and justify their abandonment because of the demands of our duties? Jesus did not do so.

20

Acknowledge with Your Life

«*When Jesus came to the region of Caesarea Philippi, he asked his disciples, "Who do people say the Son of Man is?" They replied, "Some say John the Baptist; others say Elijah; and still others, Jeremiah or one of the prophets". "But what about you?" he asked. "Who do you say I am?"*

Simon Peter answered, "You are the Christ, the Son of the living God". Jesus replied, "Blessed are you, Simon son of Jonah, for this was not revealed to you by man, but by my Father in heaven. And I tell you that you are Peter, and on this rock I will build my church, and the gates of Hades will not overcome it. I will give you the keys of the kingdom of heaven; whatever you bind on earth will be bound in heaven, and whatever you loose on earth will be loosed in heaven"».

«*Who do you say I am?*» All the synoptic writers reported on this question that Jesus asked his disciples in the region of Caesarea Philippi. It was very important for the early Christians to remember again and again whom they were following, how they were collaborating in his plan, and for whom they were risking their lives.

When we hear this question today, we tend to mouth the formulas that Christianity has fondly repeated for centuries: Jesus is the Son of God made man, the Savior of the world, the Redeemer of the human race and so on. But by just pronouncing these words is that enough to make us *followers* of Jesus? Unfortunately they are frequently formulas learned at an early age, routinely accepted, repeated meaninglessly, and affirmed but not lived.

We believe in Jesus out of custom, a pious disposition, or upbringing, but we live without understanding the originality of his life, or having heard the newness of his call, or being drawn by his mysterious love and inspired by his freedom, without any effort to follow the path he traced.

We adore him as God, but he is not the center of our lives. We acknowledge him as «Teacher», but we are not motivated by what motivated his life. We live as followers of a religion, but we are not disciples of Jesus.

In spite of their intended purpose, the «orthodoxy» of our doctrinal formulas can provide a security which at the same time dispenses with a living encounter with Jesus. There are very «orthodox» Christians who live an instinctive religiosity, but have no experience of what it is to be nourished by Jesus. They feel they are guardians of the faith, even boast of their orthodoxy, but do not know personally the dynamism of the Spirit of Jesus.

Let's not fool ourselves. Each of us has to stand before Jesus, look into our hearts, and listen in the depths of our being to his words: «*Who am I truly for you all?*» The answer to this question must be seen in the quality of our lives, more than heard in sublime words.

21

What Peter Had to Hear

MATTHEW 16: 21-27

TWENTY-SECOND SUNDAY OF ORDINARY TIME

«*From that time on Jesus began to explain to his disciples that he must go to Jerusalem and suffer many things at the hands of the elders, chief priests and teachers of the law, and that he must be killed and on the third day be raised to life. Peter took him aside and began to rebuke him. "Never, Lord!" he said. "This shall never happen to you!" Jesus turned and said to Peter, "Get behind me, Satan! You are a stumbling block to me; you do not have in mind the things of God, but the things of men".*

Then Jesus said to his disciples, "If anyone would come after me, he must deny himself and take up his cross and follow me. For whoever wants to save his life will lose it, but whoever loses his life for me will find it. What good will it be for a man if he gains the whole world, yet forfeits his soul? Or what can a man give in exchange for his soul? For the Son of Man is going to come in his Father's glory with his angels, and then he will reward each person according to what he has done. I tell you the truth, some who are standing here will not taste death before they see the Son of Man coming in his kingdom".

The appearance of Jesus in the villages of Galilee caused surprise, admiration and enthusiasm. The disciples dreamed of resounding success. Jesus, on the other hand, thought only of the will of the Father. He wished to fulfill it to the end, So he began to explain to his disciples what awaited him. He intended to go up to Jerusalem in spite of knowing he would have to suffer much there at the hands of the religious leaders. His death coincided with the plans of God as the inevitable consequence of his activities. But the Father would raise him from the dead. He would not remain aloof or indifferent.

Peter rebels against the very thought of Jesus being crucified. He doesn't want to see him a failure. He only wants to follow a victorious and triumphant Jesus. So he «*takes him aside*», he presses him and «*rebukes him*», telling him to forget what he has just said. «*Never, Lord. This shall never happen to you!*».

The reaction of Jesus is very sharp: «*Get behind me, Satan!*» He does not want to see Peter in front of him because he is «*a stumbling block to him; you do not think as God thinks, but as men think*». You do not think like the Father does, who is thinking of the happiness of all his children. You, however, only think like men do. They think only of their own welfare and interests. You are Satan incarnate.

125

When Peter in his simplicity opens himself to the revelation of the Father and acknowledges Jesus as the Son of the living God, he becomes the «rock» on which Jesus can build his church. When following human ways of thinking he tries to draw Jesus away from the way of the cross, and he turns into a tempter like Satan.

The authors underline the fact that Jesus literally says to Peter: «*Get behind me, Satan*». That is his place. As a faithful follower your place is behind me. Don't try to corrupt my life by diverting my plan to achieving power and success.

It is «satanic» to acknowledge Jesus as «Son of the living God» and not to follow him on the way of the cross. If in the church today we continue to behave the way Peter did, we also will have to hear what Peter had to hear from the lips of Jesus.

22

Gather Together in the Name of Jesus

MATTHEW 18: 15-20

TWENTY-THIRD SUNDAY OF ORDINARY TIME

«"*If your brother sins against you, go and show him his fault, just between the two of you. If he listens to you, you have won your brother over. But if he will not listen, take one or two others along, so that 'every matter may be established by the testimony of two or three witnesses' If he refuses to listen to them, tell it to the church; and if he refuses to listen even to the church, treat him as you would a pagan or tax collector. I tell you the truth, whatever you bind on earth will be bound in heaven, and whatever you loose on earth will be loosed in heaven. Again I tell you that if two of you on earth agree about anything you ask for, it will be done for you by my Father in heaven. For where two or three come together in my name, there I am with them*"».

The destruction of the Temple of Jerusalem in the year 70 caused a profound crisis in the Jewish people. The temple was the house of God. From there he reigned by imposing his Law. With the temple destroyed where could they now find his saving presence?

The rabbis responded with the meetings they held to study the Law. The famous Rabbi Hananiah who died in the year 135, stated clearly: Wherever two meet to study the words of the Law, the presence of God (the *Shekina*) is with them.

The followers of Jesus coming from Judaism reacted very differently. Matthew reminds his readers of some words that he attributes to Jesus and that are of great importance in keeping his presence alive among his followers: «*Where two or three are gathered in my name, there I am in the midst of them*».

It is not a routine meeting, called by rule or submission to an order. The atmosphere of this getting together is different. The followers of Jesus «*gather together in his name*», drawn by him, animated by his Spirit. Jesus is the reason, the inspiration, and the life of that meeting. The Risen Jesus makes himself present there.

It is no secret that the Sunday gathering of Christians is in a profound crisis. For many the Mass is intolerable. They no longer have the patience to be present at proceedings where the meaning of the symbols eludes them or they don't always hear language that touches the reality of their lives.

Some only attend Masses that are reduced to a social event, controlled and directed by church officials, where the people remain passive, locked in their silence, or give routine responses without being able to empathize with a language whose content they don't always understand. Is this called «gathering together in the name of the Lord?»

How is it possible that the Sunday gathering is disappearing and nothing happens? Isn't the Eucharist the center of Christianity? How can the hierarchy choose not to question or change anything? How can we Christians remain silent? Why is there so much passivity and a lack of will to react?

Where will the Spirit stir up meetings of two or three who will teach us how to gather in the name of Jesus?

23

What Will Become of Us without Forgiveness?

MATTHEW 18: 21-35

TWENTY-FOURTH SUNDAY OF ORDINARY TIME

« *"Then Peter came to Jesus and asked, "Lord, how many times shall I forgive my brother when he sins against me? Up to seven times?" Jesus answered, "I tell you, not seven times, but seventy-seven times".*

"Therefore, the kingdom of heaven is like a king who wanted to settle accounts with his servants. As he began the settlement, a man who owed him ten thousand talents was brought to him. Since he was not able to pay, the master ordered that he and his wife and his children and all that he had be sold to repay the debt. The servant fell on his knees before him. 'Be patient with me', he begged, 'and I will pay back everything'. The servant's master took pity on him, canceled the debt and let him go.

"But when that servant went out, he found one of his fellow servants who owed him a hundred denarii. He grabbed him and began to choke him. 'Pay back what you owe me!' he demanded. His fellow servant fell to his knees and begged him, 'Be patient with me, and I will pay you back'. But he refused. Instead, he went off and had the man thrown into prison until he could pay the debt.

"When the other servants saw what had happened, they were greatly distressed and went and told their master everything that had happened. Then the master called the servant in. 'You wicked servant', he said, 'I canceled all that debt of yours because you begged me to. Shouldn't you have had mercy on your fellow servant just as I had on you?' In anger his master turned him over to the jailers to be tortured, until he should pay back all he owed.

"This is how my heavenly Father will treat each of you un-less you forgive your brother from your heart"».

This is called «the parable of the heartless servant», because it tells of a man who, having been forgiven by the king a debt impossible to repay, cannot in turn forgive a fellow servant a trifling amount he owes him. The story seems simple and clear. However, authors continue to discuss its original mean-ing, because the unfortunate application of the parable by Matthew does not match the call of Jesus *«to forgive up to seventy-seven times»*.

The parable, which had such a promising beginning with the forgiveness of the king, ends tragically. Everything ends badly. The gesture of the king does not succeed in inspiring a more compassionate behavior in his subordinates. The for-given servant does not know how to forgive his fellow ser-vant. The other servants do not forgive him his heartlessness and ask the king to do justice. The enraged king withdraws his pardon and hands over the servant to the torturers.

For a moment it seemed a new age of understanding and mutual forgiveness could have dawned. It was not to be. In the end, compassion was revoked by all. Neither the servant nor his companions, and not even the king, heeded the plea for pardon. The king did make an initial gesture, but he too does not know how to forgive «seventy-seven times». What is Jesus trying to imply?

At times we naively believe that the world would be more human if everything were governed by order, strict justice and punishment for those who behave badly. But wouldn't we be building in this way a sunless world? What kind of society would that be where forgiveness is radically dismissed? What would become of us if God did not know how to forgive?

The denial of forgiveness seems to us quite normal and even very honorable for an offense, a humiliation or an in-justice. However, that is not what will humanize the world. A couple without mutual understanding would destroy each other. A family without forgiveness would be a hell. A society without compassion would be inhuman.

The parable of Jesus is a kind of «trap». We all think that the servant forgiven by the king *ought* to forgive his fellow servant. It is the least we could require of him. But then, isn't forgiveness *the least* to be expected of one who lives sustained by the pardon and mercy of God? We speak of forgiveness as an admirable and heroic deed, but for Jesus it is quite normal, and for us it should be likewise.

Scandalous Goodness

MATTHEW 20: 1-16

TWENTY-FIFTH SUNDAY OF ORDINARY TIME

« "For the kingdom of heaven is like a landowner who went out early in the morning to hire men to work in his vineyard. He agreed to pay them a denarius for the day and sent them into his vineyard. About the third hour he went out and saw others standing in the marketplace doing nothing. He told them, 'You also go and work in my vineyard, and I will pay you whatever is right'. So they went.

"He went out again about the sixth hour and the ninth hour and did the same thing. About the eleventh hour he went out and found still others standing around. He asked them, 'Why have you been standing here all day long doing nothing?' 'Because no one has hired us', they answered. He said to them, 'You also go and work in my vineyard'.

"When evening came, the owner of the vineyard said to his foreman, 'Call the workers and pay them their wages, beginning with the last ones hired and going on to the first'. The workers who were hired about the eleventh hour came and each received a denarius.

Following in the Footsteps of Jesus

"So when those came who were hired first, they expected to receive more. But each one of them also received a denarius. When they received it, they began to grumble against the landowner. 'These men who were hired last worked only one hour', they said, 'and you have made them equal to us who have borne the burden of the work and the heat of the day'. But he answered one of them, 'Friend, I am not being unfair to you. Didn't you agree to work for a denarius? Take your pay and go. I want to give the man who was hired last the same as I gave you. Don't I have the right to do what I want with my own money? Or are you envious because I am generous?' So the last will be first, and the first will be last"».

It was probably autumn when the season of harvesting grapes was in full swing. Jesus noticed workers in the squares who had no land of their own, waiting to be hired to earn their daily living. How could he make these poor people understand the mysterious goodness of God toward all?

Jesus tells them an astonishing parable. He spoke to them of a farm owner who hired all the workers he could. He himself came to the square of the town time and again at different hours of the day. At the end of the day's work, even though the work they had done was totally unequal, he gave everyone a silver coin. That's what a family needed to live on.

The first group hired protested. They did not complain of having received more or less money. What hurt them is that «*the owner had treated the last the same as us*». The answer of the owner to the spokesman of the group is calmly audacious: «*Are you envious because I am generous?*»

The parable is so revolutionary that even after twenty centuries we do not yet dare to take it seriously. Is it true that God is good even to those men and women who have little to show by way of merits or good works? Is it true that in his heart of a Father there are no privileges based on more or less meritorious works of those who have worked in his vineyard?

All our notions are overturned when we are faced with the free and unfathomable love of God. That is why it shocks us when it seems that Jesus bypasses the pious who are loaded with merits and goes precisely to those who are not entitled to any reward from God —sinners who do not observe the Law or prostitutes forbidden to enter the temple.

We continue with our reckoning without allowing God to be good to all. We do not tolerate his infinite goodness to all. There are people who don't deserve it. It seems to us that God should give to each one what he/she deserves and only what we deserve. It is just as well that God isn't like us. With the heart of a father, God knows how to deal with those whom we reject.

25
Gone Ahead

MATTHEW 21: 28-32

TWENTY-SIXTH SUNDAY OF ORDINARY TIME

« *"What do you think? There was a man who had two sons. He went to the first and said, 'Son, go and work today in the vineyard'. 'I will not', he answered, but later he changed his mind and went. Then the father went to the other son and said the same thing. He answered, 'I will, sir', but he did not go. Which of the two did what his father wanted?" "The first", they answered. Jesus said to them, "I tell you the truth, the tax collectors and the prostitutes are entering the kingdom of God ahead of you. For John came to you to show you the way of righteousness, and you did not believe him, but the tax collectors and the prostitutes did. And even after you saw this, you did not repent and believe him"* ».

The parable is so simple as to seem almost unworthy of a great prophet like Jesus. However, it is not addressed to the group of children scurrying around him, but to the high priests and elders of the people who harass him as he approaches the temple.

According to the story, a father asks both his sons to go to work in his vineyard. The first answers him bluntly: *«I will not»*. But he does not forget his father's request and ends up working in the vineyard. The second answers with a marvelous availability but only in words: *«I will, sir»*. Nobody will see him working in the vineyard.

The message of the parable is clear. Even the religious leaders who listen to Jesus agree. With God it is not talk that matters but deeds. To fulfill the will of the Father in heaven, what matters is not words, promises and prayers, but deeds and the way one lives every day.

What is surprising is how Jesus applies the parable. His words cannot be harsher. Only Matthew has preserved them, but there is no doubt that they come from Jesus. Only he had that kind of freedom vis-a-vis the religious leaders. *«I tell you the truth, the tax collectors and the prostitutes are entering the kingdom of God ahead of you»*.

Jesus is speaking from his own experience. The religious leaders have said «yes» to God. They are the first to speak of him, of his Law and of his temple. But when Jesus calls them to seek the kingdom of God and his righteousness, they close themselves to his message and don't heed him. They say «no» to God by resisting Jesus.

The tax collectors and prostitutes have said «no» to God. They remain outside the Law and are excluded from the temple. Still when Jesus offers them God's friendship, they listen to his call and move towards conversion. Jesus has no doubts: Zacchaeus, the tax collector, the woman who wet his feet with her tears, and so many others —all are ahead on their way to the kingdom of God.

On this path, those who are ahead are not those who make a solemn profession of faith, but those who open themselves to Jesus by taking concrete steps of conversion to God's project of bringing in the kingdom of God.

26

Dont Cheat God

�

MATTHEW 21: 33-43

TWENTY-SEVENTH SUNDAY OF ORDINARY TIME

«"*There was a landowner who planted a vineyard. He put a wall around it, dug a winepress in it and built a watchtower. Then he rented the vineyard to some farmers and went away on a journey. When the harvest time approached, he sent his servants to the tenants to collect his fruit. The tenants seized his servants; they beat one, killed another, and stoned a third. Then he sent other servants to them, more than the first time, and the tenants treated them the same way.*

"*Last of all, he sent his son to them. 'They will respect my son', he said. But when the tenants saw the son, they said to each other, 'This is the heir. Come, let's kill him and take his inheritance'. So they took him and threw him out of the vineyard and killed him. Therefore, when the owner of the vineyard comes, what will he do to those tenants*"? "*He will bring those wretches to a wretched end*", *they replied*, "*and he will rent the vineyard to other tenants, who will give him his share of the crop at harvest time*".

Jesus said to them, "Have you never read in the Scriptures: 'The stone the builders rejected has become the capstone; the Lord has done this, and it is marvelous in our eyes'? Therefore I tell you that the kingdom of God will be taken away from you and given to a people who will produce its fruit"».

The parable of the murderous tenants is so hard-hitting that it is difficult for us Christians to believe that this prophetic warning, directed at the religious leaders of his time, is intended for us as well.

The story speaks of a man who entrusted his vineyard to tenants. When harvest time comes, something surprising and unexpected happens. The tenants refuse to hand over the harvest. The owner will not gather the fruit he so much wanted.

The daring of the tenants is unbelievable. One after the other they keep on killing the servants the owner sends to collect the harvest. Now see this! When the owner sends his own son, they throw him out of the vineyard; they kill him so that they remain sole owners of everything.

What will the owner of the vineyard do to those tenants? The religious leaders who listen to the parable nervously draw a terrible conclusion: he will have them killed and give the vineyard to other tenants who will hand over to him the share of the crop at harvest time. They are condemning themselves! Jesus tells them to their faces: «*Therefore I tell you that the kingdom of God will be taken away from you and given to a people who will produce its fruit*».

In the vineyard of the Lord there is no place for those who do not produce any fruit. In his project of the kingdom of God, which Jesus announces and promotes, unworthy «tenants» cannot continue to occupy a place without recognizing the ownership of his Son, since they feel they are the owners, lords and masters of the people of God.

At times we think that this very frightening parable is intended for the time before Christ, for the people of the Old Testament, but not for us, for we belong to the New Testament and we have a guarantee that Christ will always be with us.

We're wrong. The parable refers also to us. God has no reason to bless a sterile Christianity from which he does not get the fruit he wants. He has no reason to associate himself with our inconsistencies, straying and lack of fidelity. Even now God wants the unworthy tenants of his vineyard to be substituted by a people who will produce fruit worthy of the kingdom of God.

27
On the Street Corners

MATTHEW 22: 1-14

TWENTY-EIGHTH SUNDAY OF ORDINARY TIME

«Jesus spoke to them again in parables, saying: "The kingdom of heaven is like a king who prepared a wedding banquet for his son. He sent his servants to those who had been invited to the banquet to tell them to come, but they refused to come. Then he sent some more servants and said, 'Tell those who have been invited that I have prepared my dinner: My oxen and fattened cattle have been butchered, and everything is ready. Come to the wedding banquet'. But they paid no attention and went off —one to his field, another to his business. The rest seized his servants, mistreated them and killed them.

"The king was enraged. He sent his army and destroyed those murderers and burned their city. Then he said to his servants, 'The wedding banquet is ready, but those I invited did not deserve to come. Go to the street corners and invite to the banquet anyone you find'. So the servants went out into the streets and gathered all the people they could find, both good and bad, and the wedding hall was filled with guests.

"But when the king came in to see the guests, he noticed a man there who was not wearing wedding clothes. 'Friend', he asked, 'how did you get in here without wedding clothes?' The man was speechless. Then the king told the attendants, 'Tie him hand and foot, and throw him outside, into the darkness, where there will be weeping and gnashing of teeth. 'For many are invited, but few are chosen"».

Jesus knew well how hard and monotonous life was for the peasants. He knew how they waited for the Sabbath to be relieved of work. He saw how they enjoyed themselves on feast days and at weddings. What more joyful experience could they have than to be invited to a banquet and sit down at table with acquaintances and share a meal with them?

Inspired with his experience of God, Jesus began to speak to them in a manner that surprised them. Life is not only a matter of hard work and worry, grief and boredom; God is preparing a final feast for all his children. He wants to see all of them sitting by his side at the same table, enjoying forever a life full of happiness.

Jesus didn't stop at merely talking in this way about God. He himself would invite all to his table and would eat with sinners and unwanted people. He wanted to be, in person, the extraordinary invitation of God to the final feast. He wanted to see them accepting the invitation with joy and creating together a friendly and fraternal atmosphere to prepare them decently for the final feast.

What has become of this invitation? Who announces it? Who listens to it? Where can you receive news of this feast? Satisfied with our prosperity, deaf to anything other than our own immediate interests, we do not need God. Are we not gradually getting used to living without a final hope in anything?

In Matthew's parable, when those who have properties and businesses reject the invitation, the king says to his servants: «*The wedding banquet is ready, but those I invited did not deserve to come. Go to the street corners and invite to the banquet anyone you find*». It's an unheard-of order, but it reflects the feelings of Jesus. In spite of such rejection and contempt, there will be a feast. God has not changed. He must go on inviting.

But now it is necessary to go to the street corners, where so many people hang around, those who have no lands or businesses, those whom no one has ever invited for anything. They, more than anyone else, will appreciate the invitation.

They can remind us of the ultimate need we have for God. They can teach us to hope.

28
They Belong to God and to No One Else

MATTHEW 22: 15-21

TWENTY-NINTH SUNDAY OF ORDINARY TIME

> «*Then the Pharisees went out and laid plans to trap him in his words. They sent their disciples to him along with the Herodians. "Teacher", they said, "we know you are a man of integrity and that you teach the way of God in accordance with the truth. You aren't swayed by men, because you pay no attention to who they are. Tell us then, what is your opinion? Is it right to pay taxes to Caesar or not?" But Jesus, knowing their evil intent, said, "You hypocrites, why are you trying to trap me? Show me the coin used for paying the tax". They brought him a denarius, and he asked them, "Whose portrait is this? And whose inscription?" "Caesar's", they replied. Then he said to them, "Give to Caesar what is Caesar's, and to God what is God's"*».

Very few words have been quoted as often as these: «*Give to Caesar what is Caesar's and to God what is God's*», and none have been so distorted by vested interests far removed from the Prophet who was totally dedicated to the cause, not of the Emperor but of those forgotten, impoverished, and excluded by Rome.

The incident is charged with tension. The Pharisees have retreated to plan a decisive attack on Jesus. To do so they do not come themselves, but send a «few disciples» and thus avoid a direct confrontation with Jesus. They are the guardians of the existing order, and they do not want to lose their privileged position in the society that Jesus is challenging radically.

They send them together with the supporters of Herod Antipas. Surely among them are landowners and tax collectors in charge of storing grain collected in Galilee to be sent as tribute to Caesar.

The praise they shower on him is not usually found on their lips. «*Teacher*», they said, «*we know you are a man of integrity and that you teach the way of God in accordance with the truth*». It's all a trap, but they've spoken with more truth than they intended: Jesus is entirely committed to prepare the way for God, to bring about a more just society.

He is not at the service of the Emperor of Rome; he is involved in the process of the coming of God's kingdom. He is not there to spread the Roman Empire, but to make the righteousness of God possible among his children. When they ask him whether it is right to pay taxes to Caesar or not, his answer is emphatic: «*Give to Caesar what is Caesar's, and to God what is God's*».

Jesus is not thinking of God and Caesar as two powers who can exact their rights from their subjects. As a faithful Jew he knows that «*the earth and all it contains, the world and all its inhabitants*» *(Ps.24)* belong to God. What is it that can belong to Caesar that is not God's? Only his unjust money.

If someone is entangled in the system of Caesar, he will be obliged to fulfill his obligations; but if he enters into the process of the coming of God's kingdom, he must know that the poor belong to God alone; they are his favored children. Nobody should take advantage of them. This is what Jesus teaches according to the truth. We, his followers, must withstand anyone, known or unknown to us, being sacrificed to any political, economic, religious or ecclesiastical power. Those whom the powerful humiliate belong to God, and to no one else.

29

Passion for God, Compassion for Human Beings

MATTHEW 22: 34-40

THIRTIETH SUNDAY OF ORDINARY TIME

«Hearing that Jesus had silenced the Sadducees, the Pharisees got together. One of them, an expert in the law, tested him with this question: "Teacher, which is the greatest commandment in the Law?" Jesus replied: "'Love the Lord…; your God with all your heart and with all your soul and with all your mind'. This is the first and greatest commandment. And the second is like it: 'Love your neighbor as yourself'". All the Law and the Prophets hang on these two commandments"».

When religions forget what is essential, they easily fall into pious mediocrity or moral casuistry, which not only makes them unable to promote a healthy relationship with God, but also prompts them to seriously distort or destroy the human person. No religion is immune to this risk.

The scene related in the Gospels has as its background a religious atmosphere in which religious teachers and scholars classify hundreds of rules derived from the divine Law into «easy» and «difficult», «serious» and «light», «small» and «big». It is impossible to preserve one's sanity in this web.

The question they ask seeks to retrieve what is essential, to rediscover the spirit they have lost. *«Which is the greatest commandment?»* What is of the essence, what is at the heart of religion? The answer of Jesus, as that of Hillel and other Jewish teachers, contains the core faith of Israel: *«Love the Lord your God with all your heart and with all your soul and with all your mind».*

Let no one think that this refers to emotions or feelings towards an imaginary being, or an invitation to prayers and devotions. To love God with all one's heart is to humbly recognize the ultimate mystery of life, to positively direct one's existence to fulfilling his will, and to love God as a creative and saving power who is good and loves us very much.

This way of loving God definitely gives life a new outlook, because it means being appreciative of existence at its very core; living life with gratitude; always opting for the good and the beautiful; living with a heart of flesh and not of stone; fighting whatever is against the will of God and the dignity of his children.

That's why the love of God is inseparable from the love of the neighbor. Jesus reminds us of this in these words: «*Love your neighbor as yourself*». It is not possible to really love God without becoming aware of the suffering of his children.

What sort of religion would it be where the hunger of the malnourished and the excesses of the well-fed pose no problem or scruple for the believer?

They are not wrong, those who sum up the religion of Jesus as «*passion for God and compassion for humanity*».

30
Do Not Call Anyone Father — Neither Teachers Nor Fathers

MATTHEW 23:1-12

THIRTY-FIRST SUNDAY OF ORDINARY TIME

> «*Then Jesus said to the crowds and to his disciples: "The teachers of the law and the Pharisees sit in Moses' seat. So you must obey them and do everything they tell you. But do not do what they do, for they do not practice what they preach. They tie up heavy loads and put them on men's shoulders, but they themselves are not willing to lift a finger to move them. Everything they do is done for men to see: They make their phylacteries wide and the tassels on their garments long; they love the place of honor at banquets and the most important seats in the synagogues; they*

love to be greeted in the marketplaces and to have men call them 'Rabbi'.

"But you are not to be called 'Rabbi', for you have only one Master and you are all brothers. And do not call anyone on earth 'father', for you have one Father, and he is in heaven. Nor are you to be called 'teacher', for you have one Teacher, the Christ. The greatest among you will be your servant. For whoever exalts himself will be humbled, and whoever humbles himself will be exalted"».

The Gospel of Matthew has passed down to us some very strong anti-hierarchical sayings through which Jesus asks his followers to resist the temptation to convert his movement into a group led by wise rabbis, authoritarian fathers or leaders superior to others.

These sayings have probably been shaped by Matthew to criticize the aspirations for greatness and power already noticeable among second-generation Christians but which undoubtedly echo the authentic thinking of Jesus.

«*Nor are you to be called "teacher" for you have one Teacher, while you are all brothers*». In the community of Jesus no one owns his teaching. No one has to submit doctrinally to others. We are all brothers and sisters who help each other live the experience of a God who is a father who loves to reveal himself to «little ones».

«*And do not call anyone on earth "father", for you have one Father, and he is in heaven*». In the movement of Jesus there are no «fathers», only the one in heaven. No one has to take his place. No one should set himself over the others. Any title that introduces superiority over others is against fraternity.

Few evangelical exhortations have been ignored or disobeyed as blatantly as these through the centuries. Even today the church flagrantly violates the gospel in practice. There are so many titles, prerogatives, honors and dignitaries that it is not always easy to experience others as real brothers and sisters.

Jesus imagined a church where there would not be «those above» or «those below», but instead, a church of brothers and sisters living in equality and solidarity. It is of no use to disguise the reality with the use of pious words like «service» and calling ourselves «brothers» in the liturgy. It is not a question of words but of a new spirit of mutual, friendly and fraternal service.

Will we ever see the call of the gospel fulfilled? Will we not know followers of Jesus who do not allow themselves to be called «teachers» or «fathers» or something similar? Will it be impossible to create a simpler, fraternal and loving atmosphere in the Church? What is blocking it?

31

Light the Lamps

MATTHEW 25: 1-13

THIRTY-SECOND SUNDAY OF ORDINARY TIME

«*"At that time the kingdom of heaven will be like ten virgins who took their lamps and went out to meet the bridegroom. Five of them were foolish and five were wise. The foolish ones took their lamps but did not take any oil with them. The wise, however, took oil in jars along with their lamps. The bridegroom was a long time in coming, and they all became drowsy and fell asleep. At midnight the cry rang out: 'Here's the bridegroom! Come out to meet him!'*

"Then all the virgins woke up and trimmed their lamps. The foolish ones said to the wise, 'Give us some of your oil; our lamps are going out'. 'No', they replied, 'there may not be enough for both us and you. Instead, go to those who sell oil and buy some for yourselves'. But while they were on their way to buy the oil, the bridegroom arrived. The virgins who were ready went in with him to the wedding banquet. And the door was shut. Later the others also came. 'Sir! Sir!' they said.

'Open the door for us!' But he replied, 'I tell you the truth, I don't know you'. Therefore keep watch, because you do not know the day or the hour'».

Among the first Christians there were doubtless «good» disciples and «bad» disciples. However, Matthew in his Gospel is concerned above all to remember that within the Christian community there are serious disciples who behave in a responsible and intelligent manner and «foolish» disciples who behave in a frivolous and careless way. What does this mean?

To explain this, Matthew presents two parables of Jesus. The first is quite clear. There are some who hear the words of Jesus and put them into practice. They take the gospel seriously and translate it into action. They are like the wise man who builds his house on a rock. The most responsible group of people are those who build their lives and that of the church as authentic Christians, true to Jesus.

But there are also those who hear the words of Jesus and do not put them into practice. They are as foolish as the man who builds his house on sand. His life is a disaster. He builds in the air. If it were only for them, Christianity would be a mere façade, without any real foundation in Jesus.

This parable helps us to understand the basic message of another story in which a group of young maidens go out full of joy to wait for the bridegroom and accompany him to his wedding celebration. From the start we are told that some of them are wise and some foolish. The wise take with them oil to keep their lamps lit; the foolish ones, on the other hand, don't give the matter a thought. The bridegroom delays, but arrives at midnight. The wise maidens come out with their lamps to light the way, accompany the bridegroom, and enter the wedding hall with him. The foolish ones, however, don't know how to fix their problem; their lamps have gone out, so they cannot accompany the bridegroom. When they do arrive it is late. The door is closed.

The message is clear and urgent. It is stupid to keep listening to the gospel without taking pains to make it a reality in life. This is building Christianity on sand. It is foolish to confess a faith in Jesus Christ that does not impact one's life, void of its spirit and truth; it is to wait for Jesus with the light in the lamps gone out. Jesus may delay, but we cannot delay our conversion.

32
Don't Bury Your Responsibility

∾

MATTHEW 25: 14-30

THIRTY-THIRD SUNDAY OF ORDINARY TIME

« *"Again, it will be like a man going on a journey, who called his servants and entrusted his property to them. To one he gave five talents of money, to another two talents, and to another one talent, each according to his ability. Then he went on his journey. The man who had received the five talents went at once and put his money to work and gained five more. So also, the one with the two talents gained two more. But the man who had received the one talent went off, dug a hole in the ground and hid his master's money.*

"After a long time the master of those servants returned and settled accounts with them. The man who had received the five talents brought the other five. 'Master', he said, 'you entrusted me with five talents. See, I have gained five more'. His master replied, 'Well done, good and faithful servant! You have been faithful with a few things; I will put you in charge of many things. Come and share your master's happiness!' The man with the two talents also came. 'Master', he said, 'you entrusted me with two talents; see, I have gained two more'. His master replied, 'Well done, good and faithful servant! You have been faithful with a few things; I will put you in charge of many things. Come and share your master's happiness!'

"Then the man who had received the one talent came. 'Master', he said, 'I knew that you are a hard man, harvesting where you have not sown and gathering where you have not scattered seed. So I was afraid and went out and hid your talent in the ground. See, here is what belongs to you'.

"His master replied, 'You wicked, lazy servant! So you knew that I harvest where I have not sown and gather where I have not scattered seed? Well then, you should have put my money on deposit with the bankers, so that when I returned I would have received it back with interest. Take the talent from him and give it to the one who has the ten talents'. For everyone who has will be given more, and he will have an abundance. Whoever does not have, even what he has will be taken from him. And throw that worthless servant outside, into the darkness, where there will be weeping and gnashing of teeth"».

The parable of the talents is an open story that lends itself to different interpretations. In fact, commentators and preachers have frequently interpreted it in an allegorical sense for different purposes. It is important to focus on the behavior of the third servant, because he takes up the greater part of the space and of our attention in the parable.

His behavior is strange. While the other servants are busy multiplying the assets of their master, the third doesn't bother to do anything other than hide the talent he received in the ground to keep it safe. When the master returns, he condemns him as a negligent and lazy servant who hasn't understood anything. How does he account for his behavior?

This servant does not feel identified with his master or his business. At no time is his behavior prompted by love. He doesn't love his master. He fears him. It is precisely that fear which moves him to seek his own security. He himself explains everything: «*I was afraid and went out and hid your talent in the ground*».

This servant does not understand his real responsibility. He thinks he is living up to the expectations of his master, keeping his talent secure though unproductive. He does not know what it means to be actively and creatively faithful. He does not involve himself in the projects of his master. When the latter arrives, he tells him clearly: «*See, here is what belongs to you*».

When we think that Christianity has reached the stage where the only and main thing is to preserve it, and not as something to search and live for by proclaiming his project of the kingdom of God, we forget our true responsibility.

If we never feel called to follow the demands of Christ beyond what has always been taught and commanded; if we risk nothing to form a life more faithful to Jesus; if we stay free of any conversion that may complicate our lives; if we do not assume responsibility for the kingdom as Jesus did, seeking «new wine in new bottles», it is because we need lessons in the kind of active and creative fidelity to which the parable invites us.

33
A Strange Trial

MATTHEW 25: 31-46

OUR LORD JESUS CHRIST THE KING

> «*"When the Son of Man comes in his glory, and all the angels with him, he will sit on his throne in heavenly glory. All the nations will be gathered before him, and he will separate the people one from another as a shepherd separates the sheep from the goats.*
>
> *"He will put the sheep on his right and the goats on his left. Then the King will say to those on his right, 'Come, you who are blessed by my Father; take your inheritance, the kingdom prepared for you since the creation of the world. For I was hungry and you gave me something to eat, I was thirsty and you gave me something to drink, I was a stranger and you invited*

me in, I needed clothes and you clothed me, I was sick and you looked after me, I was in prison and you came to visit me'.

"Then the righteous will answer him, 'Lord, when did we see you hungry and feed you, or thirsty and give you something to drink? When did we see you a stranger and invite you in, or needing clothes and clothe you? When did we see you sick or in prison and go to visit you?' The King will reply, 'I tell you the truth, whatever you did for one of the least of these brothers of mine, you did for me'.

"Then he will say to those on his left, 'Depart from me, you who are cursed, into the eternal fire prepared for the devil and his angels. For I was hungry and you gave me nothing to eat, I was thirsty and you gave me nothing to drink, I was a stranger and you did not invite me in, I needed clothes and you did not clothe me, I was sick and in prison and you did not look after me'.

"They also will answer, 'Lord, when did we see you hungry or thirsty or a stranger or needing clothes or sick or in prison, and did not help you?' He will reply, 'I tell you the truth, whatever you did not do for one of the least of these, you did not do for me'. Then they will go away to eternal punishment, but the righteous to eternal life"».

The sources are unmistakably clear. Jesus lives wholeheartedly devoted to those who need help. He is incapable of deliberately ignoring anyone. He is no stranger to the sufferings of others. He identifies with the most insignificant and helpless, and he does whatever he can for them. For him, compassion comes first. It is the only way for us to be like God: «*Be merciful as your Father is compassionate*».

Why should we be surprised that when speaking of the last judgment, Jesus presents compassion as the ultimate and decisive criterion to judge our lives and our identification with him? Why should we be surprised that he presents himself as identified with the poor and the unfortunate in human history?

In Matthew's account all the nations appear before the Son of man, that is, before Jesus, the compassionate one. There is no difference between the chosen people and pagans. Nothing is said of various religions and cults. Only something very human is mentioned, which everyone can understand: what have we done for all those who suffered in life?

The evangelist does not trouble himself with details of a trial. What stands out is a double dialogue that sheds a strong light on our present day and opens our eyes to see that, ultimately, there are two ways to react to those who suffer: we either sympathize with and help them, or we walk away and abandon them.

The speaker is a judge who is identified with all the poor and needy: «*Every time you help one of these my little brothers, you did it to me*». Those who have come to help a needy person, have come to him. So they have to be with him in the kingdom: «*Come, blessed of my Father*». Next he turns to those who have lived without compassion: «*As long as you did not do it to these little ones, you did not do it to me*». Those who have turned away from those who suffer, have turned away from Jesus. It makes sense that he now says to them: «*Depart from me*» and «*Go away…*».

Our life is on trial NOW. Do not wait for any future trial. It is now that we either meet or turn away from those who suffer. It is now that we either meet or turn away from Christ. Our life is judged here and now.

Other Feasts

1
God Loves this World

JOHN 3: 16-18

THE HOLY TRINITY

> «*"For God so loved the world that he gave his one and only Son, that whoever believes in him shall not perish but have eternal life. For God did not send his Son into the world to condemn the world, but to save the world through him. Whoever believes in him is not condemned, but whoever does not believe stands condemned already because he has not believed in the name of God's one and only Son"*».

One can regard Jesus from various points of view. He can be seen as an historical problem, a great religious leader, a dogma, the inspirer of a way of liberation. John, the evangelist, invites us to accept him as «the best gift» God has given the world.

Jesus is speaking to a Jewish teacher called Nicodemus. They do not discuss the problems arising from conflicting opinions on Jewish Law. Jesus instead draws attention to issues of which they hardly talk in Israel: how to be «reborn» to a new life, and the path to follow to gain eternal life.

All of a sudden Jesus says something that transcends all human discourse and sums up in awe-inspiring words the whole mystery enshrined in him: «*For God so loved the world that he gave his one and only Son, that whoever believes in him shall not perish but have eternal life*».

What can the men and women of today, all of us, feel on hearing these words, attracted as we are by only our immediate need of total well-being, and so skeptical of promises of a distant eternal life? What meaning can the love of God have for us in a society full of ambitions, goals and struggles so opposed to love?

The words of Jesus highlight the immense and universal love of God. It could not be otherwise. God has loved the «world», not only Israel, not only the church, or only Christians. He has sent his Son, not to condemn but to save; not to destroy, but to give eternal life. Whether we know it or not, the world exists, evolves, and keeps going under the loving gaze of God.

The best way to know something of the Mystery of Love which sustains the world is through Jesus himself. When we know the Son, we are able to see, touch, and sense the Father's love for all his children. When we see his life we are able to sense the Spirit that animates God.

All the actions, symbols, words, doctrines, objectives and strategies of Christianity must be born of, nourished by, and reflect that mystery of the love of God for the whole world. If not, religion shuts itself in on itself, the Christian message loses much of its genuine meaning, and we can even invent practices, customs, and ways of living far removed from the original truth of Christianity.

2
A Crucial Experience

JOHN 6: 51-59

THE HOLY BODY AND BLOOD OF CHRIST

> «"I am the living bread that came down from heaven. If anyone eats of this bread, he will live forever. This bread is my flesh, which I will give for the life of the world". Then the Jews began to argue sharply among themselves, "How can this man give us his flesh to eat?" Jesus said to them, "I tell you the truth, unless you eat the flesh of the Son of Man and drink his blood, you have no life in you. Whoever eats my flesh and drinks my blood has eternal life, and I will raise him up at the last day. For my flesh is real food and my blood is real drink. Whoever eats my

flesh and drinks my blood remains in me, and I in him. Just as the living Father sent me and I live because of the Father, so the one who feeds on me will live because of me. This is the bread that came down from heaven. Your forefathers ate manna and died, but he who feeds on this bread will live forever". He said this while teaching in the synagogue in Capernaum».

It is quite natural that the celebration of the Mass has kept on changing through the centuries. Theologians and liturgists have been highlighting some aspects and downplaying others, depending on the age in which they were living. The Mass has provided a framework for the celebration of coronations of kings and popes, as well as to render homage or commemorate war victories. Musicians have turned it into a concert. People have integrated it into their devotions and religious customs. After twenty centuries it may be necessary to remember some of the essential features of the last Supper of the Lord, exactly as it was remembered and lived by the first generation of Christians.

As the basis of this supper there is something that will never be forgotten: his followers will not be left orphans. The death of Jesus will not be able to sever their communion with him. No one should feel the void of his absence. His disciples will not be left alone at the mercy of historical avatars. At the center of every Christian community that celebrates the Eucharist is Christ, alive and active. Here lies the secret of its power.

The faith of his followers is nourished by him. It is not enough to be present at Mass. The disciples are invited to «eat». To nourish our attachment to Christ, we need to gather together to listen to his words and to let them enter our hearts, and to come forward to «communicate» with him, identifying ourselves with the way he lived. No other experience can bring us more solid nourishment. We must not forget that to «communicate» with Jesus is to «communicate» with someone who has lived and died, «given» totally for others. Jesus emphasizes this. His body is a «body given» and his blood is «blood shed» for the salvation of all. It is a contradiction to «communicate» with Jesus and to egoistically resist involving ourselves with anything except our own interests.

There is nothing as central and crucial for the followers of Jesus as the celebration of this supper of the Lord. That is why we should take such great care in its celebration. Properly celebrated, the Eucharist molds us, keeps uniting us with Christ, nourishes us with his life, keeps us in close touch with the Gospels, invites us to live in a spirit of fraternal service, and keeps alive in us the hope of a final reunion with him.

3

156 *Peter's Confession of Christ*

MATTHEW 16: 13-20

FEAST OF STS. PETER AND PAUL

> «*When Jesus came to the region of Caesarea Philippi, he asked his disciples, "Who do people say the Son of Man is?" They replied, "Some say John the Baptist; others say Elijah; and still others, Jeremiah or one of the prophets". "But what about you?", he asked. "Who do you say I am?" Simon Peter answered, "You are the Christ, the Son of the living God". Jesus replied, "Blessed are you, Simon son of Jonah, for this was not revealed to you by man, but by my Father in heaven. And I tell you that you are Peter, and on this rock I will build my church, and the gates of Hades will not overcome it. I will give you the keys of the kingdom of heaven; whatever you bind on earth will be bound in heaven, and whatever you loose on earth will be loosed in heaven". Then he warned his disciples not to tell anyone that he was the Christ*».

Jesus was conversing with his disciples in the region of Cae-sarea Philippi, not far from the source of the Jordan. The episode occupies a prominent place in the Gospel of Matthew. He probably does not want his readers to confuse the «churches» originating with Jesus, with the Jewish synagogues where all sorts of opinions about him were current.

The first thing they must clearly understand is about who is at the center of the church. Jesus asks his disciples directly: «*You, who do you say that I am?*» Peter answers: «*You are the Messiah, the Son of the living God*». He understands that Jesus is not only the awaited Messiah; he is the Son of the living God, the God who is life, source and origin of all that lives. Peter grasps the mystery of Jesus in his words and deeds that bring healing, pardon and new life to the people.

Jesus commends Peter: «*Blessed are you… because only my Father in Heaven has revealed that to you*». No human being of flesh and blood can awaken that faith in Jesus. Those things the Father reveals to the little ones, not to the learned and clever. Peter belongs to that category of the simple followers of Jesus who live with a heart open to the Father. This is the greatness of Peter and of every true believer.

Jesus then makes a solemn promise: «*You are Peter and upon this rock I will build my church*». Not just anyone builds this church. It is Jesus himself who builds it. It is he who calls together his followers and unites them around himself. The church is his. It is born of him. Jesus is not a fool who builds on sand. Peter will be a rock in this church, not because of the solidity and firmness of his temperament, for even though he is honest and passionate he is also inconstant and inconsistent. His strength lies in his simple faith in Jesus. Peter is the prototype and promoter of true faith in Jesus.

This is the great contribution of Peter and his successors to the church of Jesus. Peter is not the Son of the living God, but the son of Jonah. The church is not his, but of Jesus. Jesus alone occupies the center. He alone builds it with his Spirit. But Peter calls us to live open to the revelation of the Father, not to forget Jesus, and to keep the church focused on the true faith.

4
Do Not Confuse Jesus with Anyone

∽

MATTHEW 17:1-9

THE FEAST OF THE TRANSFIGURATION

«*After six days Jesus took with him Peter, James and John the brother of James, and led them up a high mountain by themselves. There he was transfigured before them. His face shone like the sun, and his clothes became as white as the light. Just then there appeared before them Moses and Elijah, talking with Jesus.*

Peter said to Jesus, "Lord, it is good for us to be here. If you wish, I will put up three shelters—one for you, one for Moses and one for Elijah".

While he was still speaking, a bright cloud enveloped them, and a voice from the cloud said, "This is my Son, whom I love; with him I am well pleased. Listen to him!" When the disciples heard this, they fell facedown on the ground, terrified. But Jesus came and touched them. "Get up", he said. "Don't be afraid". When they looked up, they saw no one except Jesus.

As they were coming down from the mountain, Jesus instructed them. "Don't tell anyone what you have seen, until the Son of Man has been raised from the dead"».

According to the evangelist, Jesus takes Peter, James and John alone with him up to a high mountain, and there he was transfigured before them. It would seem that it was these three who, when he spoke to them about it, greatly resisted the idea that Jesus was destined to be painfully crucified. Peter even tried to get him to forget these absurd thoughts. James and John kept asking him for the first places in the kingdom of the Messiah. It is precisely before these three that Jesus will be transfigured. They need it more than anyone.

The scene, recreated with a lot of symbolism, is magnificent. Jesus appears before them clothed in the glory of God himself. At the same time, Moses and Elijah, who according to tradition have been snatched from death and live close to God, appear in conversation with him. Everything prompts us to discern the divinity of Jesus, crucified by his enemies but raised from the dead by God.

Peter reacts quite spontaneously. *«Lord, it is good for us to be here. If you wish, I will put up three shelters —one for you, one for Moses and one for Elijah».* He has not learned anything. On the one hand, he places Jesus on the same plane and in the same category as Elijah and Moses, giving to each one his shelter; on the other hand, he continues to resist walking the hard road Jesus shows him. Instead, he wants Jesus to hold on to the glory of Mount Tabor, away from the passion and cross of Calvary. God himself solemnly corrects Peter: *«This is my Son».* He is not to be confused with anyone else. *«Hear him»,* even when he speaks to you of the way of the cross which ends in resurrection.

Only Jesus radiates light. All others, prophets and teachers, theologians and the hierarchy, doctors and preachers, we all live in his shadow. We must not confuse anybody else with Jesus. He alone is the beloved Son. His is the only Word to which we must listen. All the others must lead us to him. And we must listen to it even today, when he tells us to carry the cross of these times.

Success harms us as Christians. We have even been led to believe that it is possible to have a church faithful to Jesus and his project of the kingdom, without opposition, without rejection, and without the cross. Yet, today we are far more likely to be faced with the possibility of living as crucified Christians. It will do us good. It will help us to regain our Christian identity.

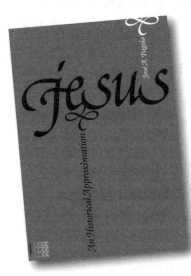

Following in the Footsteps of Jesus
Meditations on the Gospels for Year A

This book was printed on *thin opaque smooth white Bible paper*, using the *Minion* and *Type Embellishments One* font families.

This edition was printed in D'VINNI, S.A., in Bogotá, Colombia, during the last weeks of the ninth month of year two thousand ten.

Ad publicam lucem datus mense septembre in nativitate Sancte Marie